THE COMPLETE GUIDE TO
FISHING

THE COMPLETE GUIDE TO
FISHING

THE FISH, THE TACKLE, & THE TECHNIQUES

JOHN BAILEY

Foreword by
MARK SOSIN

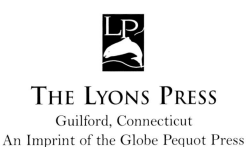

THE LYONS PRESS
Guilford, Connecticut
An Imprint of the Globe Pequot Press

CONTENTS

FOREWORD 7

–

THE 21ST-CENTURY ANGLER 8

–

GETTING STARTED 18

–

THE FISHER NATURALIST 26

–

BAIT FISHING 40

–

LURE FISHING 52

–

FLY FISHING 62

–

BAIT FISHING IN STILLWATERS 76

–

BAIT FISHING IN RIVERS 86

–

LURE FISHING TECHNIQUES 98

–

FLY CASTING TECHNIQUES 108

–

FLY FISHING TECHNIQUES 114

–

BASS FISHING 124

–

SEA FISHING 136

–

MOVING FORWARDS 146

GLOSSARY OF KNOTS 156 • INDEX 158 • ACKNOWLEDGEMENTS 160

Publishing Manager: Jo Hemmings
Editorial/Design: Design Revolution
Production: Joan Woodroffe

Printed and bound by Kyodo Printing Co (Singapore) Pte Ltd

The Library of Congress Cataloging-in-Publication Data is available on file.

FOREWORD

John Bailey and I learned about fish, fishing, and the environment on opposite sides of a great ocean, and yet those lessons proved to be strikingly similar. Within the first few pages of his *Complete Guide to Fishing*, one begins to sense John Bailey's love of the sport and deep-rooted appreciation of the natural world that shoulders stream and pond, river and estuary, and even the majestic oceans.

Think of John as a teacher and educator, willing to share his knowledge along with his philosophy of fishing with everyone who exhibits even a passing interest. He begins by telling you about the camaraderie and common bond that fishing provides whether you travel to the corners of the Earth to pursue this sport or merely probe and prowl the waters at your doorstep.

For the beginner, he quickly warns that fishing provides both mental and physical exercise that breeds an inner desire to master the skills and techniques. The thought that angling could be considered sedentary and contemplative at any time waxes foreign to John. For him as for me, it ranks as a consuming passion. And both of us believe strongly that one should pursue a multitude of species using different types of tackle rather than limiting interest to a single one.

The details he passes along on fish behaviour and how to identify differences in what a fish does remind me of my own efforts early in my career to understand this fascinating subject and then write about it so others could benefit. As an angler becomes more in tune with his environment, the enjoyment from every day on the water is magnified.

Perhaps it's time to pause for an instant to admire the beautiful colour photography that adorns every page of this book. The pictures tell their own story and illustrate every part of John's writings to perfection. These vivid illustrations showcase fish species from around the world along with tackle, techniques, and the appeal of environments that sing a siren's song.

In reading this book and studying its lessons, the secret lies in grasping the similarities of fishing around the world rather than the differences. All of these methods can be applied on this side of the great pond as well as on the other. We may not have the same species, and there could be a few tackle items that don't match ours, but John Bailey teaches us to fish successfully and thrive in the outdoors.

Through the passages of *The Complete Guide to Fishing*, I marvel at how far afield John has roamed and the broadness of his background. He has challenged species in remote parts of the world that I could only dream of pursuing. Reading about them fuels my interest and desire even more. Nothing etches the sport of angling more indelibly in one's mind than firsthand experience with a plethora of the world's greatest gamefish—bass, trout, pike, salmon, tarpon, sea bass, bonefish and dozens of others. These are memories that even the sands of time can never erase. And for those of us who have yet to take on these species, John's carefully chosen words make us that much more knowledgeable about them.

Subtly, but in a strong, positive way, John laces the concept of catch-and-release fishing through every chapter. From his world travels, he recognizes how fragile the world's fisheries can be and knows that at least a partial solution stems from every angler keeping only what is essential and releasing everything else alive so that it will be there tomorrow.

No matter how many times I went back to read or review a particular part of the book, I found myself in agreement with its message and the particular thoughts and techniques that John found essential. To me, this points out that fishing knows no borders or boundaries. Regardless of species, the basics seldom vary. One can easily transfer the tactics necessary for one species to another in a different part of the world.

John Bailey shares the thought that fishing experts don't really exist. All of us are students of the game and eventually discover that the more we learn, the less we really know. The addiction of angling strengthens because no two experiences are the same and no two days on the water identical.

Once you finish reading *The Complete Guide to Fishing*, I think you'll agree that a day with John Bailey would be a meaningful experience. I sincerely hope we get that chance to fish together.

MARK SOSIN
Boca Raton, Florida

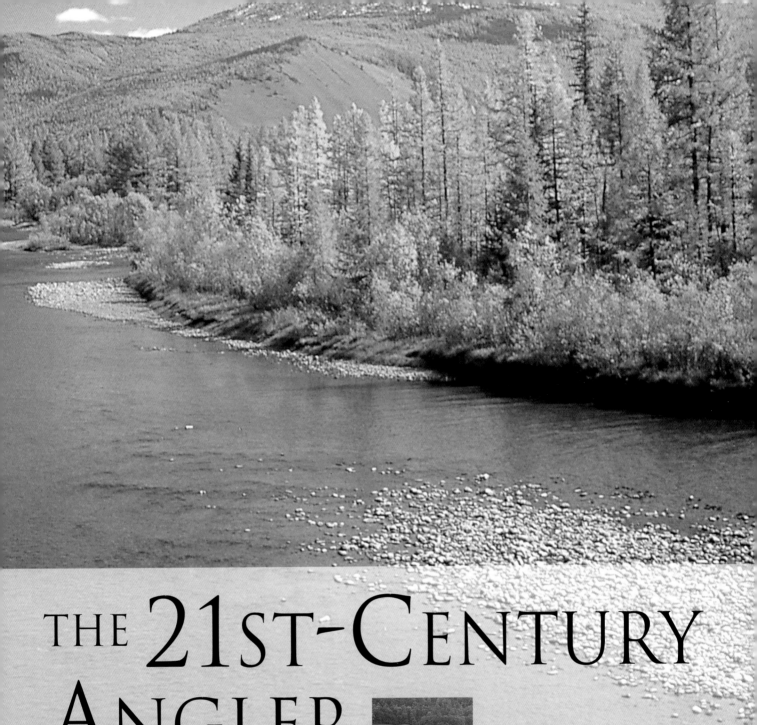

THE 21ST-CENTURY ANGLER

THE 21ST-CENTURY ANGLER

I TRULY DON'T THINK THAT YOU'LL EVER REGRET BUYING THIS BOOK OR TAKING UP FISHING AS A PASTIME – A SPORT THAT HAS GIVEN MY OWN LIFE SUCH THRUST AND DIRECTION.

▾ THE MIGHTY MAHSEER
Travel is very much a part of the 21st-century angler's world, and the travelling angler can catch beautiful silver mahseer like this in many rivers in the Indian sub-continent.

The great thing about fishing is that it is such a multi-dimensional activity, so much so that it is hard to know where to begin – or stop – singing its praises. Above everything else, fishing gets you into some wonderful environments. I look back through the 40 years that I've been a passionate angler and I think of the beautiful places that I've been fortunate to visit. Lakes of total peace and serenity. Gushing rivers, full of vitality and life. Lonely marshes. Streams running fresh from snow-capped mountains. Heart-stopping sunrises and sunsets. I

> THE SALMON POOL
Fishing with complete concentration on a trout and salmon river on Exmoor, England. A run of small summer salmon has ascended the river and is now lying in a deep, sleepy pool where one might just be tempted, even in full sunlight.

think too of the amazing wildlife I've seen – kingfishers actually perching on my rod, badgers taking bread almost out of my hand as dusk begins to fall. An otter whistling downriver in the dawn light. And when I've been travelling and fishing abroad, the rumble of a bear, the bellow of an elephant, or the swooping displays of fish eagles.

Fishing also breeds comradeship, and I have an address book absolutely crammed with the very best of companions from the past and present. Men – and women – with whom I've shared some of the very best times of my life, out in the open, by the side of water, often under the stars, around a campfire. Stories swapped. Theories presented and ideas hammered out. Laughter. Shared successes. Mutual, passionate interests. There's an old phrase about the 'brotherhood of the angle', and it couldn't be more true: it doesn't matter where you fish, either home or away, you'll find friends that you never forget.

◄ A SCOTTISH LOCH AT DAWN
The rising sun over this stunning loch will warm the water, bring on a fly hatch, and soon it will be a trout fisherman's heaven.

FISHING SKILLS

There's a huge misconception about fishing that, somehow, it's a relaxing sport, and not a taxing one. But once you really get into fishing, you'll find that there are just as many physical skills to learn as you need for soccer, baseball or golf.

You'll want to know how to cast an imitation fly 20 yards (18m) or more, sometimes into a wind, and so lightly that it hardly disturbs the water as it settles. Learning how to work a lure – an imitation fish of wood, plastic, or metal – so that it looks exactly like a living, struggling fish can be quite a challenge. You'll also learn to trot a float – that is, letting it drift with the current a hundred yards (90m) or more – yet remain in complete control. You'll experience the excitement of feeling the line for a biting fish, and interpreting all the signals that are transmitted. In short, fishing is an active, mobile sport, and the 21st-century angler is somebody who really goes with the flow, fishes actively, and is a long way from the stereotyped image of a sandwich guzzler rooted to his basket.

You will find, too, that the fishing tackle itself, the tools of your trade, can be extremely beautiful. There's a lot to appreciate in exquisite workmanship. Modern rods are breathtakingly feather-light. With luck, if you choose properly, you'll build a relationship with your rod, reel and floats, and a real intimacy will begin to flourish. The physical satisfaction of using the gear properly will bring you much pleasure. You might find artificial flies fascinating, or you might even begin to tie your own, and suddenly the long cold winter evenings become golden times when you feel that you can smell the warm summer evenings to come.

◤ GREENLAND DREAM

Experiencing all the drama of Greenland. This angler has been pulled out into the rapids by a battling sea-run Arctic char. The wilder the fish, the more hairy the battle.

◥ ON THE MOVE

Many anglers prefer traveling light and fishing many places along the river during the course of the day, rather than sitting still and waiting for the fish to come to them. It's your choice, but remember that fishing is all about fun.

◄ RIVER BOURNE
In my view, you just can't beat getting out there into the water itself. Wear chest waders and take care, but then enjoy that powerful feeling of being at one with the water.

WATER SAFETY GUIDELINES

1 Never wade in water that is so cloudy that you can't see the bottom.

2 Make sure that you never wade in too strong a current.

3 Never wade so deeply that you begin to feel afraid.

4 Always have a wading stick with you – this third 'leg' can be a real lifesaver.

5 Wear Polaroid glasses when wading – you will gain a more secure foothold if you can see the bottom contours.

6 Always wear a buoyancy aid when either wading or out in a boat.

7 A whistle is good for attracting attention in case of an emergency.

8 When setting out in a boat, always make sure that you have a pair of oars and rollocks, even if you think your engine is reliable.

9 Always set off into the wind on a big water. If the engine should fail, it's easier to row home with the wind at your back.

10 Always let somebody on shore know where you're going on a large water and approximately what time you expect to be back.

11 Always check the weather forecast before setting out onto a big, exposed water. Dangerous conditions can whip up in a matter of minutes.

◄ WADING BASICS
Wading really pays dividends when it's vital to get close to the fish. Line control is tighter and you can present a small bait accurately. The peaked cap cuts down on surface glare and allows better vision through the water's surface.

⚘ WORLD AT YOUR FEET
Fishing is a sport with endless horizons. Here I am surveying a river on the borders of China that has probably never been fished by a European before. The thrill of such moments is immense but probably no greater now than it was for me 30 odd years ago when I approached a new park pool or an English river.

FISHING AS A CHALLENGE

The methods that you will begin to pick up are mind-consuming and fascinating. Fishing is like a huge chess game, always demanding new approaches. Every water, every lie, every day brings a new challenge. You'll soon find that if you approach every situation in the same way, your successes will begin to falter. It's vital to think, to experiment, and to stay one step ahead of the game. But, perhaps above all, the modern angler appreciates the fish themselves. The creatures that we pursue are fascinating. Each species has its own habits and idiosyncrasies, and to succeed as an angler, you have to immerse yourself in their natural history. There is a whole aquatic world waiting to be discovered. Fish are absolutely, achingly beautiful.

Moreover, it's a secret beauty, a loveliness that's only really appreciated by the fisher. You will surely come to marvel at the wonder of the fish that you catch. Look carefully at each and every one of them. Note how their scales all have different patterns and sheens. Admire the shape of the fish, consider how it is perfectly adapted to its own particular environment. Examine the fins, see how delicate and yet strong they are, and how they are streaked with the most vividly coloured rays. Fish are priceless creatures, not some commodity that you buy in your weekly shop from a superstore.

You are on the threshold of a magical new departure in your life, so try to enjoy every privileged and thrilling moment that you spend by the waterside.

➤ AMAZING GRACE
Fish are simply beautiful creatures. Look at the colouration on this splendid Arctic char, fresh from the sea and driving on towards its spawning grounds. It was held a moment in the glittering sunlight before being returned to the water to continue its role in the world.

◄ SECRET BEAUTY
Another stunningly beautiful fish, this is a grayling coming to hand in an Asian river. Look at the huge dorsal fin on its back and the fabulous colours along its flanks. Those of us who fish are granted access to a totally secret, magical world.

THE FISHING CODE

Let's return for a moment to rules and regulations. Most thoughtful and experienced anglers have their own personal codes, as well as those imposed upon them by clubs and organizations.

Now, I'm not going to insult you with clichéd advice about leaving litter, lines and so on. But it's a good idea to collect other people's litter up at the bankside. Take a bin liner with you so you can clean up your own little patch of other people's refuse. This might sound like a chore, but many foresighted anglers are now doing this; litter breeds litter and the less there is around the waterside, the less the likelihood of it being dropped in the future.

Make sure that you always take any discarded nylon line home with you. There used to be a school of thought that you could burn it at the bankside but there's little point in that. Simply bin it.

Shut all gates. If you are driving across fields, keep to the tracks. It's important that anglers and farmers get on well together. I know through bitter experience that lack of co-operation can lead to tears. Remember that straightforward-looking grass is the beef farmer's crop just as much as a field full of cereal, so take great pains to avoid harming it.

▼ THINK OF THE FISH
To prevent stress, avoid taking a fish from the water itself. If you want to hold the fish for a quick photograph, try to do so just above the water so that it's only in the air for a matter of seconds.

FISH CARE

RULE 1 Always wet your hands before touching a fish.

RULE 2 Wherever possible, remove barbs from hooks. This makes unhooking 10 times easier.

RULE 3 If possible, do not use trebles on spinners but only a single hook.

RULE 4 Try, whenever possible, to unhook a fish in the water and let it go free without ever leaving its environment.

RULE 5 Think very carefully whether you need to land a fish in a net and take it away from the waterside for photography or weighing. Only do this for important specimens.

RULE 6 If a fish is tired after its struggle, support it gently in the shallows with its head facing up-river so oxygen passes through its gills. This can take many minutes, so don't be impatient.

RULE 7 Never keep fish in a keep-net. They suffer both mental stress and physical discomfort – sometimes so great that death results.

RULE 8 Don't be greedy. If you think you have caught enough fish, pack it in for the day and let them rest and recover.

RULE 9 Always make sure that a fish swims away from you as pristine as the moment that you hooked it.

RULE 10 When game fishing, if you want to take a fish for the table, pick a male rather than a female. This especially applies to a female salmon, whose eggs are so precious.

Watch out for anybody who might be poaching. Illegal sales of big fish are now big business, and, as most of us have mobiles now, a quick call to a club secretary or even the police does not come amiss if you have real suspicions – though, of course, don't put yourself in any danger.

Most vital of all, do watch out for any sign of pollution. If you see the water becoming tainted or, even worse, fish in distress then make an immediate call to the club secretary or the local Environment Agency. Remember that anglers are the guardians of the countryside, so take this vision of yourself seriously from the beginning.

◄ SHAD MAN!
I've hooked this shad out in quick water and, as it tired, brought it back into the shallows where I can kneel beside it, take out my forceps, and slip the hook out.

▼ GENTLY CRADLED
This is the way to look at a fish, when the clear water is washing it, enhancing all its colours. Once it is unhooked, hold it in the water facing upstream until you can feel its strength returning. Once it has started to flex its fins and work, allow it back into the current.

GETTING
STARTED

Getting Started

I T'S VERY HARD TO SAY WHICH PART OF THIS BOOK YOU'LL FIND THE MOST INTERESTING — THE FLY FISHING, THE BAIT FISHING OR EVEN SEA FISHING. NATURALLY, A LOT DEPENDS ON WHERE YOU LIVE.

If you're in a mountainous area with fast-flowing streams, then you'll probably be destined to fish for trout. On the other hand, if your home is in a lowland, urban environment, it's very probable that you'll do more bait fishing. Obviously, you've got to make a start somewhere and the most obvious places are close to home. As your interest in fishing grows, you'll probably do more travelling, spread your wings and begin to appreciate all the styles of fishing that are available to you.

I personally think it's a great shame when anglers become blinkered into one discipline. For example, it's very common for an angler simply to pursue trout all his or her life and totally ignore the interest in pike, say, or carp. Equally, the carp

specialist often overlooks the delight of fishing a roach river with a stick float. Only by fishing for as many species as you possibly can, in as many water types, and using as many different methods will you become a truly rounded angler.

First, you've got to serve your apprenticeship. Where do you begin?

You've got to check that your chosen water is actually in season. Traditionally, waters worldwide have had closed seasons to allow fish to spawn in peace. Different types of fish spawn at different times, and the

> ➤ REALISTIC DREAMS
As a beginner, it's generally good sense not to set your sights on the really exotic species. Roach (like this fine specimen), and pan fish if you're in America, make sensible early choices.

➢ IN THE KNOW
There is an old phrase 'the brotherhood of the angle', and it's true that most anglers welcome beginners to the sport or visitors to a new water with helpful advice. Just don't be afraid to ask.

closed seasons have been designated to protect them all. So, before you begin to fish, you need to do your research. Remember, though, wherever you live, there's likely to be some kind of fish in season that you can target, whatever the month.

Whatever part of the country you choose to fish, it is likely that you will need at least one, if not two, licences. As a general rule, you will have to buy a national or state rod licence and, very frequently, you will then require permission from the owner of any specific water. It

⋏ A WILD BROWN TROUT
Although trout are nearly always caught on a fly, there are times when they may respond very well indeed to a float-fished worm. This is especially true when the water is very coloured, and you want to fish for them at long range. Always check the local rules though.

⋨ MONSTERS
Remember that when you catch a small pike, it could grow on to be a monster like this one. My good friend Johnny holds a 47 pound (21kg) pike caught from the slightly saline Baltic Sea in Sweden. It was taken on a lure.

sounds confusing, but don't worry, any tackle shop will give advice.

It really pays, though, to think about joining a local angling club. You won't have any difficulty locating these – the world is honeycombed with them. The club will have a good sprinkling of waters within easy radius of your home and, above all, it will probably have outings and evenings that will help you to develop confidence and knowledge.

As you progress, you might want to join a syndicate; groups of anglers come together to pay large amounts of money to a landowner in return for access to desirable waters. However, these can be costly, so it's generally best to wait until you've got more experience.

◄ SPORT FOR ALL
Fishing really is a sport for everybody, young and old, male and female. If you are a real beginner, it makes sense to fish in the nicest possible weather: undoing tangles is never fun, but it's all the worse in wind and rain.

▼ PAN OF GOLD
You just never know what the next bite might bring you. Taken in Scandinavia, this is a stunning golden crucian carp, a sub-species that is very rare but highly sought after.

RULES AND REGULATIONS

Wherever you begin your fishing, always check the local rules and regulations. Every different water and each different club imposes its own rules. Some, for example, will not allow live baiting, night fishing, or whatever takes the committee's fancy! Don't worry too much. This isn't bureaucracy gone mad, it's simply a way of protecting the water, the fish themselves and the enjoyment of those that fish there.

Now for equipment. It's important to build up a relationship with a tackle dealer. If you live in a large urban area, there will probably be quite a choice. Tackle shops can seem forbidding places at first – there will be gear in every corner, and you probably won't have a clue what any of it is for. There'll be muttered conversations at the counter, which sound like nothing but gobbledegook. But don't worry, I know exactly what it's like, and there's nobody alive who is expert at everything. My advice is to visit all

the tackle shops and see where you get the friendliest welcome. Do you think the tackle dealer is going to advise you impartially, or will he try to get you to buy an expensive rod that has been on his hands for quite a while? The wise tackle dealer will know that a beginner like yourself could easily become a valued customer in years to come and, if he's got any sense, he'll do his very best to make sure that you start off on the right footing.

Mail order is, however, a quickly growing branch of the tackle trade. Some mail order companies aren't particularly fantastic – their stocks are limited and their service is slow. However, the biggest and best mail order operations are very slick indeed. It's a really good idea to get hold of their catalogues at the very least, as this gives you a really good overview of what tackle is available and also what it's for. Before you put in an order, speak to someone about the tackle that you are considering buying and see if their advice is detailed and considerate.

A LOVELY BARBEL
No wonder Joy looks so happy with this beautiful fish. Notice, though, how she is holding it, close to her body and low to the ground, with her hands well away from its stomach and any vital organs.

ON THE WILD SIDE
Odds are that you'll begin fishing on local pools and rivers, but the sport can take you to some very dramatic places, such as this river in eastern Siberia. The trout fishing here is superb but James, in the foreground, has done his homework very solidly on the reservoirs and rivers of England and Europe.

THE RIGHT CLOTHING

Think very carefully about your clothing; it's likely that you'll need at least a few bits of specialist gear.

Things aren't too difficult in the summer – all you'll need is a lightweight waterproof in case a sunny day turns into a thundery one. The real problem comes in the winter. If you're cold, you can't simply just concentrate on your fishing. You'll feel miserable and it won't be long before you set off for home. Winter clothing has, however, come along in huge strides over the last 10 years or so. Thermal boots and gloves mean comfort for the extremities. Multi-layered, synthetic underclothes are also a boon, especially topped by fleeces and 100%-effective waterproofs. Many of the manufacturers now claim that you can fish out in temperatures to minus 40 degrees centigrade and still feel warm… mind you there'd be six foot of ice over the fastest flowing river by that time, wouldn't there?! When it comes to buying your winter clothing, it really does pay to buy the best that you can afford. If there's any weakness or any vulnerability in your gear, you can guarantee a cold, snow-bearing northerly will show it up.

COOL AND WATERPROOF

Footwear is also vital. In the summer, if the money is available, I don't think you can do better than lightweight Gore-Tex chestwaders. These allow you to get out into a river or over a firm lake bed without fretting over wet feet. They also provide a great deal of protection from heavy dew falls and, if it should come to rain, all you'll need is a lightweight top to make sure you stay as dry as a bone. Gore-Tex is breathable, which means that you can walk for miles in hot temperatures

and not experience any perspiration whatsoever. Try that in traditional rubber chestwaders, and you'll create your own little pond in each boot.

In the winter, you can either keep your lightweight Gore-Tex chestwaders and wear warm thermals underneath, or buy neoprene waders. These really do keep you very cosy indeed, and the elements can hardly reach you at all – even when you're seated on a wet and muddy river bank.

➢ SUMMER WANDERINGS
There are those blissful summer days when you know there isn't going to be a shower in sight and you can wander the riverbank wearing pretty much whatever you want. Life doesn't get better than this, and you can travel for miles, totally unencumbered.

⅄ DRESSING FOR THE JOB
Chest waders make sense if you're wading into the water – especially the modern lightweight ones that allow you to walk miles without expiring with the heat. Make sure you have a waterproof jacket for showers and Polaroids for real penetration through the surface glare.

THE COMFORTABLE ANGLER

It's very important to realize that unless you're comfortable and at peace with yourself, you just won't be able to concentrate properly on your fishing. In fact, you'll pretty soon make an excuse to pack up and go for home, and you won't catch many fish that way! Here are just a few pointers to help you feel comfortable at the waterside, so that you can get on with the job of enjoying your fishing.

1 Don't drink alcohol – it acts as an initial stimulant but leaves you cold in winter after the first flush of euphoria. In the summer heat, it is far better to take soft drinks, mineral water or juices.

2 In the winter, supply yourself with plenty of hot drinks to maintain inner warmth. The early and late summer months can also prove to be very chilly.

3 Don't stint on energy producing food, especially if you're fly fishing, lure fishing, or any style of fishing that demands physical activity. If you're feeling hungry, then you'll soon be thinking of home.

4 Even if you don't wear it, always take a hat with you. Remember that in winter a great deal of heat escapes through your head and even in summer, if your head gets wet, you'll soon begin to feel chilly.

5 Unless it's a baking summer's day, always make sure that you keep your body and, in particular, your hands and feet, bone dry. Once your fingers become wet and icy, then all chance of effective fishing will disappear.

6 Be especially careful of river banks in icy winter conditions or even in wet, slippery summer ones. Believe me, there is absolutely nothing worse than falling in when temperatures are below freezing… I know, it's happened to me on a couple of occasions and the second time I was lucky to escape with my life.

7 If there are mosquitoes or midges about, don't forget a net or insect repellent lotion – you just cannot fish if you're harassed by insects.

8 If you're planning a very long stay at a water – after carp, for example – make sure that you've got something comfortable to sit or lie on. Once your body begins to ache, your concentration soon vanishes.

THE FISHER
NATURALIST

THE FISHER NATURALIST

SO WHAT ABOUT THE FISH THEMSELVES? WHAT OF THESE CREATURES THAT WE ARE PURSUING, HOPING EVENTUALLY TO CATCH? IT'S ALL TOO EASY TO IMAGINE THEM AS ALIEN TO US IN EVERY WAY – THEY'RE COLD-BLOODED, THEY BREATHE THROUGH GILLS, HAVE A SCALY SKIN, AND ARE COVERED IN A PROTECTIVE SLIME.

In all these ways they are indeed different from us, but there are many similarities between fish and humans. It's important to realize that fish have very acute eyesight, that they can feel vibrations just as easily as we pick up sounds, that they have a very well developed sense of taste, and that they learn rapidly through experience. Fish are not fools – they are complicated packages of subterranean life. The fisher who forgets this often ends up fishless.

It's equally vital to recognize that all fish species behave in slightly different ways. The experienced fish watcher knows that each and every species has its own distinctive characteristics that immediately mark it out as unique and individual. In Europe, for example, roach and rudd look alike and are both shoal fish. Rudd, however, tend to hang much higher in the water, frequently dimpling the surface for insects. Roach, on the other hand, generally

A FISH OF THE SUMMER
Tench have very tiny scales indeed, and are covered by a thick protective slime of mucus. Note also the very big fins that help give the tench its power. The red eye is quite small, as tench feed largely through touch and smell.

THE SHOALING INSTINCT
Shoals of rudd spend a great deal of their time in mid-water, close to the surface. They are nervous, darting fish, with shoal members continually looking around for the appearance of any threatening predator.

work in mid-water, or towards the bottom. Bream, too, are shoal fish, but they are almost always lying deep. Carp will move together in small groups, not really shoals, and then break away for solitary feeding. One predator, the pike, is generally a loner, and yet perch, walleye, and zander, which are also fish eaters, tend to operate in packs. To make things even more confusing, brown trout generally have a territory all to themselves, whereas rainbow trout will frequently cruise together in large numbers.

We often talk about human beings having body language and the same is certainly true for fish. As your experience as a riverside observer grows, you will soon be able to distinguish between the distressed fish, the sulking fish, and, vitally for the angler, the fish that's very shortly going to be looking for food.

⋏ BEWARE!

This is what the rudd, or any other small prey fish, sees when a hunting pike approaches. The eye directly focused, the mouth about to open, the fins quivering and the body tensed, ready for an attack.

⋎ BOTTOM FEEDERS

Bream are gentle, bottom feeding fish that generally swim in shoals. Their large, deep bodies don't allow for swift acceleration but this shape does make it difficult for predators to attack.

➤ THE STALKER
When you're watching fish, try to make use of any cover that you can find. Trees, bushes and rushes will disguise your scary shadow.

POLAROID GLASSES AND BINOCULARS

Polaroid glasses are essential for looking through the surface layer of the water and seeing how the fish are behaving. Binoculars are also a huge boon, allowing you to zoom in on a far distant carp or a close-up fly hatch.

RULE 1 Always buy the best that you can afford. Quality does count.

RULE 2 Ask advice before purchasing and, if possible, test at the waterside.

RULE 3 With Polaroid glasses, always choose strong frames and, if possible, scratchproof lenses.

RULE 4 You'll find that different colour lenses are particularly suited to different light values. A good, general all-round colour is light bronze.

RULE 5 Attach your Polaroid glasses to a cord so that they hang around your neck. It's all too easy to lose several pairs during a single year!

RULE 6 Try to choose a relatively light pair of binoculars. If they're too heavy, you'll find that you leave them at home or in the car, rather than taking them to the bankside where they really make a difference.

RULE 7 Make sure that the binoculars offer adequate magnification and let in enough light – 8 x 32 or 8 x 40 are perfect models.

RULE 8 Always make sure that the binoculars you buy are waterproof for obvious reasons!

➤ COMPARATIVE SIZES
Remember that binoculars can make fish seem bigger than they really are. It's a good idea to have a scale alongside to make comparisons. For example, is there a feather floating near a fish that can give you a clearer idea of its size?

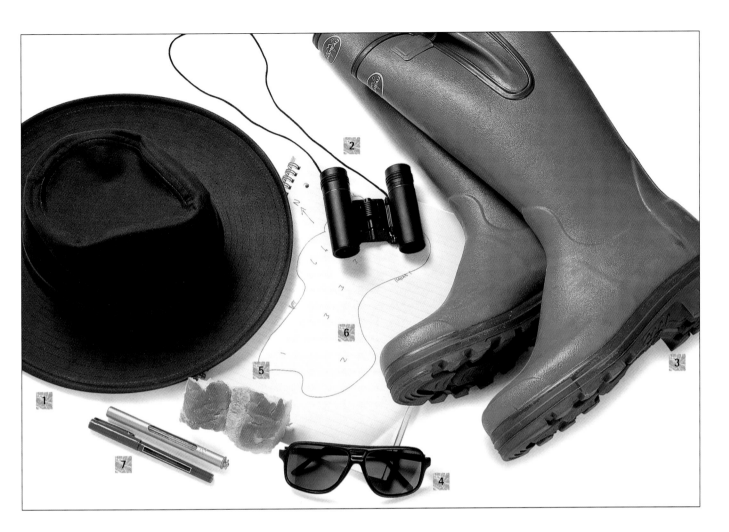

GETTING TO KNOW A WATER

If you can manage it, never go to a new fishing water with a rod in your hand, as this just makes you too eager to start. It's far better to make that first visit with Polaroid glasses, binoculars, a sketch pad, and an open mind. Give yourself time to relax and watch what is going on about you. The better you get to know a water, the more it will reveal its secrets to you.

The sketch pad enables you to make a rough map of the whole water and detailed sketches of particular areas. When preparing your fishing strategy at home, these will remind you where deep water lies, where there are shallows, which bays face north or west, and where there are reed beds. Never discard any single piece of information that you might pick up. Everything adds

to your complete understanding of the water to be fished.

A thermometer is a very useful tool for the angler, because temperature plays a much more vital role in the life of a fish than it does for us. Being cold-blooded, they tend to adapt their entire life to the temperature of the water around them.

As a rule, the colder the water, the more torpid the fish. As the water warms up, their body mechanisms kick-start, and they begin to feed again. A thermometer tells an angler how the fish may be behaving. For example, if river temperatures drop much below 6 or 7°C (42-46°F) in the winter, then it's unlikely you will find barbel feeding, and it's best to fish for pike. If water temperatures rise much above 30°C (86°F), then you are probably better off fishing in the cool of the dawn.

OBSERVATION EQUIPMENT

1 **HAT** *A broad brim keeps the sun off your head and out of your eyes.*

2 **BINOCULARS** *These allow you to scan the water surface for signs of fish topping.*

3 **BOOTS** *Always choose a pair that are warm, well-fitting and waterproof.*

4 **POLAROIDS** *Reducing glare, these are your windows into the fish's world.*

5 **BREAD** *Many fish species adore the simple, ordinary shop-bought loaf.*

6 **SKETCH PAD** *A simple map can prove invaluable when planning your strategy.*

7 **PEN AND THERMOMETER** *These are essential aids. The water temperature is an important piece of information.*

⊼ LILIES

Carp and lily-beds almost invariably go together. Carp like the muddy, yet firm texture in which the plants grow, and all manner of fish enjoy hoovering the stems and pads of the plant for aquatic organisms.

◁ TARKA'S RETURN

It is good to see otters returning to waters all over the northern hemisphere, for they are a sure sign that fish stocks are in a healthy state. The best time to sight otters is at dawn, when their night's hunting is all but over and they are on their way home.

LOCATING THE FISH

The first job of importance is to locate the fish within the water. This might sound blindingly obvious, but it's not always easy. You've got to remember that fish aren't scattered about like currants in a cake. Rather, they live tightly packed in closely defined areas. And there's always a good reason for it. In general terms, fish are looking to find homes that provide them with food and security. So, for example, small fish will nearly always hang around reed beds or areas of heavy weed. Such places give them bountiful food supplies as well as the opportunity to hide whenever a predator comes into view. To take another example: imagine a huge featureless pit that has just been excavated and filled with water. There are absolutely no contours or places to hide. However, if a dead tree falls into the water, within days a pike or group of bass will be lurking among its sunken roots and branches, using it as an ambush area. The message is clear: look for anything in the water that

can provide the fish with a hiding place or an ample food supply. This may be a bed of freshwater mussels, or a colony of insects. The more you look, the more you'll see, and the better the picture of the water that you build up in your mind's eye.

⋏ TREASURE ISLAND

Always look out for islands, especially when a lot of bushes have fallen over into the water. All kinds of fish enjoy the shelter and security of such places, especially in the heat of the day when they want to hide up and rest rather than roam and feed. A long cast, close into the island's margins, can often bring a bite when everything else fails.

⋖ SANCTUARY

Always look very carefully around underwater tree roots and trailing branches, as fish love to hang there, escaping the full force of the current and also finding a lot of food. The fish pictured here is a big chub on an English river.

STALKING TIPS

1 It's always best to have the sun behind you as it will light up the water that you are looking into and there will be less light reflecting into your eyes from the water. Remember to wear a sun visor above your Polaroids to cut out unwanted light.

2 At the same time, bear in mind that your shadow can really ruin your chances of success as a fisher, so try to stand behind a tree or amidst reeds – this will break up your outline. Don't wear white or bright clothing.

3 To remain unnoticed, always move slowly. Vibrations travel well in water, so step gently.

4 In the summer, rub yourself well with insect repellent because fish watching often calls for long periods of immobility amongst mosquito-infested reed beds!

LEARNING TO SEE FISH

Actually, physically seeing fish can often be a problem until you get used to it. Fish are built to be as near invisible as possible, or they would be picked off by the many predators above and below the water. Fish, generally, move gently and subtly, and blend in seamlessly with their surroundings, so your eye needs to be trained to pick up very diffuse images indeed. The best tip is to look very, very carefully indeed at a given piece of water. Really concentrate on it, and look out for anything that catches the eye. You might suddenly see a glint or perhaps a shadow. Home in on these little telltale signs, and the chances are you'll begin to pick out a scale, an eye or the profile of a fin. Once you've done that, focus even more sharply and the whole fish will begin to come into view. It's like magic and a skill that you'll always treasure.

⋏ POND LIFE

A typical European pond scene – the rudd in mid-water looking up to the surface for a struggling fly, perhaps, while the tench keeps lower, its mind set on a meal of bloodworms.

⋎ CAMOUFLAGE

Modern floats today tend to be made out of plastic but, when it comes to camouflage, it's difficult to beat an old quill. Look how this merges in perfectly with the lily stems.

FISH SELF-DEFENCE

1 Many fish prey on the fry of other species – and even their own! Because it reduces their losses, small fish will come together in huge shoals. By darting around, they confuse a predator and make it difficult for it to pick out a single target and home in for the kill.

2 Camouflage is another important weapon in the protective armory. Many fish will adapt their colour to suit their background, and the individuals of any particular species can vary widely in appearance, depending on their habitat.

3 Hiding is another technique used, especially by prey fish. They will utilize any object in a water that gives them cover and security.

4 Experience is also vital. Fish do learn fast, and they'll recognize anglers as threats just as much as an otter, a kingfisher, or a pike.

⋏ EAGLE EYE

You just can't beat getting an aerial view of any water. A good angler is frequently a good climber but do take care, especially in winter, when tree branches can be slippery and rubber boots don't have the very best of grips.

⋎ BATTLE OF WITS

Here you can just see the shadowy, secretive shape of a fish gliding under the surface, wondering whether to go down to feed or not. Perhaps it's afraid of the float – if you placed it closer to the lily-pads, it would be less obtrusive.

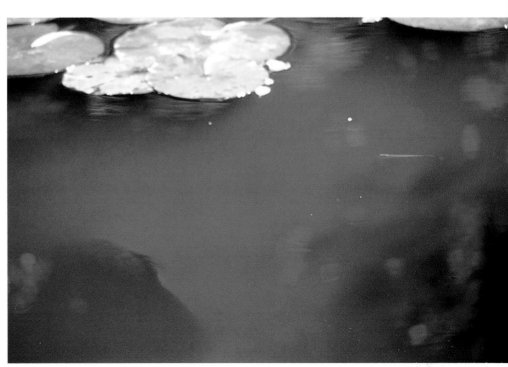

⬈ THE EASY LIFE
Carp love to bask in sheltered, warm areas
when the sun is out. Look for them in reedy
places where the breeze has pushed a scum
onto the surface.

⬋ PERCH ATTACK
These two perch are in typical attack mode.
When perch begin to feel the pangs of
hunger, they move up through the layers of
water watching out for small fish swimming
above them.

READING BODY LANGUAGE

As you become more adept at seeing fish, you'll soon find that there is more to learn from them than the simple fact that they are there. In no time at all, you'll discover how to interpret their body language.

Take, for example, a carp that is barely moving, simply hanging under the surface film, occasionally stretching a fin out into the sunlight. This is a fish that is not feeding at all. It is simply browsing, half asleep, enjoying the sunshine, and no amount of effort on your part is likely to persuade it to take a bait. When, on the other hand, you see a carp moving purposefully, often dropping down toward the bottom, then you know this is a fish with food on its mind, one that's becoming catchable.

What about a pike, lying doggo on the bottom of a lake, with perhaps silt or leaves building up around it? This is a fish that's fed heavily and is lying comatose, digesting its prey. Once you see that pike rise a few inches from the bottom, however, often angled upward like a cannon, then you know it's ready to spring, ready to attack, and catchable once more if you make the right approach.

⋏ DEAD TO THE WORLD
Pike feed very irregularly, especially in cold water when prey fish take a long time to digest. For most of their lives, pike will simply lie comatose on the bottom waiting until they feel hunger once more.

FEEDING TERMS

Fisher-people over the years have concocted all manner of terms and phrases to describe how fish feed. Here are some of the most common ones.

BUBBLING – many fish send up bubbles as they root around on the bottom. Tench produce strings of tiny bubbles, whereas bream produce fewer, larger ones. In time, you'll get to know which bubble goes with which species.

FRY FEEDING – you'll often see whole carpets of tiny fish, or fry, lift from the surface, especially toward the late summer and autumn. These are almost certainly being harried by groups of predatory fish such as trout, perch, or even pike that have come together for the feast.

NYMPHING – this describes fish, trout in particular, that are feeding on nymphs (see page 122) as they scuttle looking for cover, or rise to the surface to hatch. You will often just see the white of the inside of the mouth as the jaws open and close.

SMOKE SCREENING – sometimes you'll see a vast area of silty mud rise to the surface. This will be made by a group of big fish, probably carp, rooting around in the mud for minute organisms.

READING THE WATER

Of course, sometimes the water becomes too cloudy to see any fish, especially after heavy rain. When this happens, you have to look for the sort of signs that fish give off.

In shallow areas, you might see fin tips breaking the surface and vortices as the strong bodies weave beneath. This could well be a shoal of bream feeding on bloodworm. Shaking reed stems are often a sign of foraging carp. A shower of fry, breaking the surface like a hail of needles, is a real give-away that a predator is in the area. A big cloud of mud mushrooming to the surface indicates a big fish burrowing. Small puffs of silt coming up here and there might suggest a shoal of smaller fish at their dinner table.

The more you watch, the more you realize that fish lead very ordered lives and have patrol routes that they use from day to day, often at predictable times. This helps the fisher no end to prepare an ambush and to bait up the right area.

The only times that the fish behave out of character is during their spawning periods, when they will frequently migrate long distances and come together in great numbers. If you can manage it, always try to get to the waterside when spawning is about to take place. Leave your rod at home and give the fish the peace they need at this vital time of the year, but do try to witness this thrilling sight. Spawning carp can literally flatten a reed bed, and river fish will come together in their thousands on the gravel beds and beat the dawn water to a foam. Nature in the raw can make exciting viewing.

▼ PISCATORIAL PROFESSORS

Carp are possibly the most inquisitive of all fish and will immediately begin to investigate any new bait that you care to offer them. Mind you, they're also very cunning, and will inspect baits carefully for any sign of a hook, line or lead before committing themselves.

⋏ FRENZY

When carp spawn, they can flatten whole reed beds and turn a crystal lake into a chocolate one within an hour. The full fury of their spawning can whip the water to a foam and you can often hear their activities a quarter of a mile away or more. It's not unusual to find a carp on the grassy banks, lifted clear of the water altogether in its exertions.

⋖ USE THE CLUES

It's important to be able to recognize bubbles on the surface. Some of them are simply marsh gas, escaped from the bottom of mud and leaves. Fish, however, often make bubbles as well when they feed. For example, tench bubbles are very small, whereas carp bubbles tend to be larger and frothier. Fishing, as you can see, is very largely about detective work.

BAIT
FISHING

Bait Fishing

BAIT FISHING IS SIMPLY PRESENTING SOMETHING EDIBLE ON A HOOK IN AN AREA OF WATER WHERE FISH ARE FEEDING. THERE ARE MANY HUNDREDS OF DIFFERENT BAIT TYPES, AND THEY ARE ATTRACTIVE TO ALL SORTS OF FISH AROUND THE WORLD. IN EUROPE, TENCH, CARP, ROACH, BARBEL, BREAM AND CHUB ARE AMONG THE FAVOURITE SPECIES OF BAIT FISHERS. PRIZED FISH IN THE STATES INCLUDE PAN FISH SUCH AS BLUE GILLS, SUNFISH AND SMALL MOUTH BASS.

⋀ FEEDERS
A fine barbel comes towards the bank, caught on a swim feeder rig. Swim feeders are good at getting samples of the hook bait down to the river bottom where the fish are feeding. This can be difficult otherwise in a quick current.

You can start bait fishing by buying a quite cheap 11 foot (3.5m) rod, a fixed spool reel, 4 or 5 pound (1.8–2.2kg) line, floats, split shot, a few lead weights, hooks, a loaf of bread or a pint of maggots, and a

ticket to your local water. With this modest skeletal kit, you can begin to catch your fish for a relatively small monetary outlay. Taking it just a little further though, what you choose to buy in the first instance

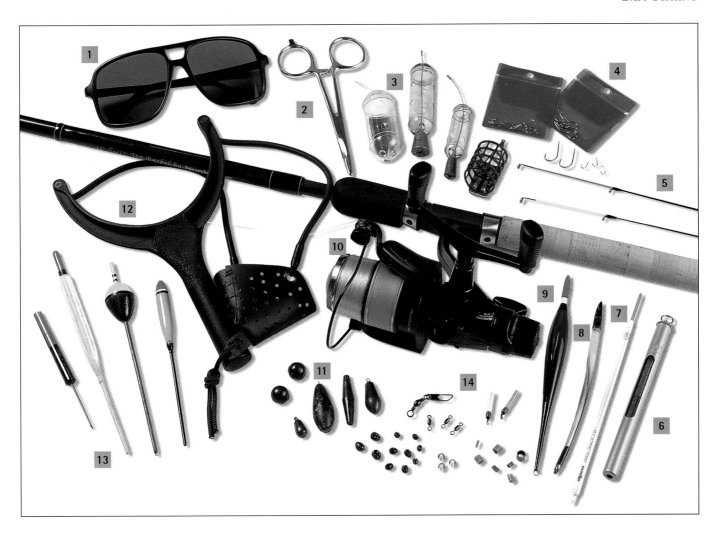

rather depends on the sort of water you will be fishing, and the type of fish you hope to catch.

There are three basic rods that you should think about looking at for your introduction to bait fishing.

The first rod to consider is a float rod, designed to cast a light bait with a float on the line to indicate a bite. This rod will be between 12 and 13 feet (3.6–4m) long, and will weigh perhaps 6 or 7 ounces (170–200g).

You might also want to use a swim feeder, especially if you're fishing for any bottom feeders. For this technique you'll need a rod between 10½ and 12 feet (3.2–3.6m) long. Go for an average-strength feeder rod that's capable of taking lines between 3 and 8 pounds (1.4– 3.6kg) breaking strain – this way you can fish for anything from roach right through to the bigger species.

BAIT FISHING EQUIPMENT

1 POLAROID GLASSES *These allow you to see beneath the surface glare.*

2 FORCEPS *Use forceps for easy hook removal and flattening hook barbs.*

3 SWIM FEEDERS *A selection of these will suit different waters and conditions.*

4 HOOKS *Always take a selection of hook sizes for different types of bait.*

5 QUIVER TIPS *These offer good bite indication.*

6 THERMOMETER *It's always useful to know the water temperature, and many experts take a thermometer.*

7 WAGGLER FLOAT *A transparent waggler float for still or slow waters.*

8 QUILL FLOAT *This is perfect for close-in fishing on a lake.*

9 AVON TYPE FLOAT *This type of float is for fast water and big baits.*

10 FIXED SPOOL REEL *A modern fixed spool reel – the best of buys.*

11 LEDGER WEIGHTS *A selection of these, including bombs and bullets.*

12 BAIT CATAPULT *This allows you to fire small bait (e.g. maggots) far from the bank.*

13 RIVER FLOATS *A selection of river floats, together with a baiting needle.*

14 TERMINAL TACKLE *Shot to weight the line, swivels to prevent the line twisting, beads and float rubbers are part of the kit.*

A SPECIALIST CHOICE

Thirdly, you might decide you need some sort of specialist rod in case you want to do a certain amount of lightish carp fishing, pike fishing, or perhaps even some heavier river work. In this case, a rod of about 12 feet (3.6m) in length, with a test curve of around about a 1½ pound to a 1¾ pound (700–800g), is ideal. Test curve is the term used to indicate the strength of the rod. It means that a 1¾ pound (800g) force will bend the rod tip to something like 90 degrees.

With these three rods, you should be able to tackle the vast majority of situations, and it's only really the mega stuff that would be out of reach.

You should always buy a known brand. This need not be expensive, but it should mean reliability and good back-up service. Don't rush into a decision. Hold as many rods as possible and, if you can, actually try them at the riverbank. The rod should feel balanced so that it doesn't tire you, but feels more like an extension to your arm.

AN ALL-ROUND REEL

The choice of reels is, again, overwhelming but, at an early stage in the game, I'd discount centre-pin reels (useful for fishing rivers), multiplier reels (good for very heavy work like pike fishing on big waters), and closed-face reels (useful for very fine lines in stronger winds). What you really need is a good fixed-spool reel and there are many different types to choose from. Go for an established brand, and one that balances your rod or rods perfectly.

◄ GUERRILLA WARFARE
A low, clear, summer river. Fish afraid of their own shadows. It's now that the slowest, most careful approach to the water is called for. Keep low. Use any bankside cover available and watch those stones. A careless footfall will send shock signals all the way down the river.

BAIT FISHER'S GLOSSARY

BITE – the action of a fish sipping in the bait on the hook.

FLOAT – a float is a pencil-shaped object that is made of plastic, feather quill, or reed. The float is attached to the line above the bait. Its purpose is to suspend the bait at different levels in the water, and also to signal when a bite has taken place.

GROUNDBAIT – bait fishers often use groundbait to attract fish into the area and to get the fish feeding without suspicion. A groundbait can be samples of the actual hook bait. Alternatively, it may be a cloud made of something like breadcrumb, with flavourings and scents added to it.

HOOK LENGTH – bait fishers generally use a main line, which can be quite strong, and then a slightly finer piece of line – generally around about 3 foot (1m) or so in length – that is attached to the hook. This is known as the hook length.

LEDGER WEIGHT – a ledger weight is a piece of lead that can vary in shape but which is attached to the line to take the bait quickly down to the bottom and keep it there – even in a quick flowing current.

POLE – some bait fishers – especially those looking for large numbers of smaller fish – do not use a conventional rod and reel. Instead they use a pole. This can be very long – often 30 foot (9m) or more in length – and made out of the lightest carbon fibre. The line is simply attached to the top ring, and then the float and bait are flicked out. Small fish are then swung in without being played off a reel.

PRE BAITING – very often bait fishers seeking big, crafty fish will put samples of the hook bait into the swim over a period of several days before actually fishing. The suspicions of the fish are relaxed and they begin to look for samples of the hook bait.

QUIVER TIP – a quiver tip is a very fine insert of carbon fibre into the top of a conventional rod. The line from the quiver tip to the bait is maintained under tension so the quiver tip bends just a little. When a fish picks up the bait, the quiver tip either pulls right round or leaps back straight.

RUN – this is generally a carp fishing term. When a big fish such as a carp picks up a bait, it generally runs off with it – hence the terminology.

SPLIT SHOT – split shot are simply pieces of metal put onto the line beneath the float. These make the float cock in an upright position and also help take the bait down to the required depth. These were originally made out of lead, but they are now made of non-toxic metal, since lead has been shown to be harmful to wildfowl.

STRIKE – the act of lifting the rod and pulling the hook out of the bait into a biting fish.

SWIM – a particular area of water chosen by the bait fisher to groundbait and fish intensely. A swim is often situated close to a feature such as lily beds or deeper water.

SWIM FEEDER – a swim feeder is a small container made out of plastic and put on the line – somewhere just above the hook length. It contains samples of the hook bait that then dribble out of the feeder once it has hit the bottom. The idea is to entice fish and lull their suspicions.

TROTTING – trotting is simply allowing the current to take your float along the river, thus exploring a great deal of water and giving you the possibility of covering many different fish. It's possible to trot anything up to 300 feet (90m) or more away.

⌄ PREPARING TO CAST
Note the hand movements here as you're preparing to cast a bait out into the water. Make sure that the rod always feels comfortable in your hand, and see how the index finger is gripping the line so it won't fall off the spool when the bail arm is released.

⌄ SET TO GO
The line is now gripped tightly to the rod butt as the left hand moves back the bail arm. Once the bail arm is fully off, the line can flow off the spool freely. The cast can then be made by swinging the rod back, flicking it towards the target spot and releasing the line.

⌄ FEATHERING THE LINE
As the line flows off the reel, you may well want to slow the bait down as it threatens to overshoot the chosen target. Placing your finger on the spool allows you to do this. Once the cast is complete, turn the handle of the reel to flick the bail arm over the spool.

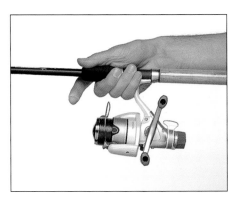

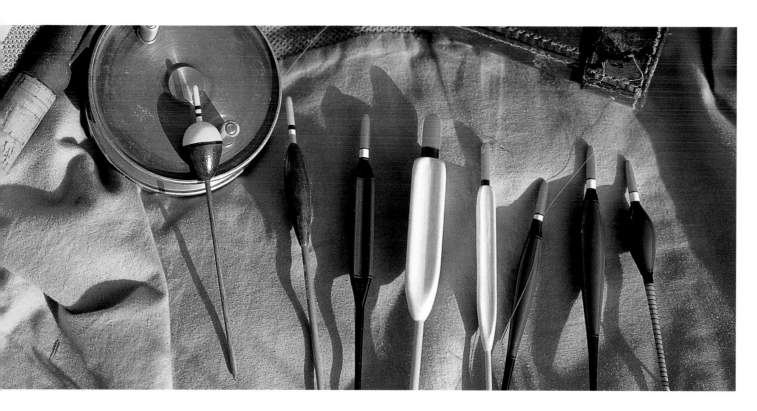

▲ RIVER DELIGHT
Once you get really experienced, you might think about using a centre-pin reel, which makes trotting a float very easy indeed. The line comes off it perfectly and you're in constant contact.

REELS AND FLOATS

In fact, buy the rod and reel together and make sure they fit together and work nicely. As a rule of thumb, the rod with the reel attached should balance nicely on your finger, somewhere towards the head of the rod handle.

Don't buy too small a reel: it should be able to hold 300 feet (90m) of 7–10 pound (3–4.5kg) line easily. Anything smaller than this will make pike or carp fishing very difficult indeed. Ask the tackle dealer whether the reel has a smooth clutch – this is important for playing a fish. It's a good idea for the reel to have spare spools since you could very well need different strengths of line to suit different fishing conditions. You will probably need line of around 3 or 4 pound (1.3–1.8kg) breaking strain, 6 to 8 pound (2.7–3.6kg) breaking

strain, and perhaps a spool of 10 pound (4.5kg) line. Once again, this should cover pretty well anything you're likely to need. As a rough rule of thumb, use a 3 pound (1.3kg) line for smaller fish, the 8 pound (3.6kg) line for barbel, and the 10 pound (4.5kg) line for carp and pike – this will do you until you build up more experience.

Always buy line of a reputable brand: economizing on line makes very bad sense indeed, as it's the one thing that connects you with your fish.

Now, you'll need some floats, and I would suggest a few stick floats for river fishing and some wagglers for lakes and pools. Buy a selection of different sizes and do remember that you've got to put enough split shot on the line so that the float cocks and sits nicely in the water and is cast easily. It's better to use a float slightly too heavy than one too light because you'll have less trouble casting and controlling it. Look for floats with a variety of different coloured tips so that you can see them against different coloured backgrounds.

CHOOSING TACKLE

1 Don't be intimidated by your tackle dealer! Even though he ought to be an expert, he should be very willing to help a beginner in a down-to-earth, uncondescending fashion.

2 If you live in a city, try to visit as many tackle shops as you can so that you can compare prices and the advice given. If at all possible, go and choose your first outfit with a friend who already fishes.

3 Do not buy secondhand tackle advertised in the local newspaper. The chances are that it will be flawed in some way, or the owner wouldn't want to be getting rid of it. It's not necessarily wise to listen to the hundred plausible excuses.

4 Decide your budget and stick to it: it's only too easy to be enticed into buying the latest and swishest models – these aren't necessary at this early stage.

5 Do not, however, skimp on quality when it comes to lines and hooks. These, after all, are the major link between you and your fish.

▲ STILLWATER FLOATS
The two floats on the left are wagglers and you attach them to the line by the bottom end only. The two floats on the right are designed for lighter, close-in work.

▲ RIVER FLOATS
A selection of river floats. The one on the left, a stick float, is perfect for fine work for smaller fish in clear water conditions. The yellow-topped float would be ideal for a worm bait, and the remaining two would work well in fairly fast flowing conditions.

➤ FASTWATER FLOATS
A selection of river floats. Note how the three floats on the left all have fluted bodies. This allows them to grip the current well and not be pushed off course. The other two floats are perfect with big baits in streamy conditions.

⋏ TURNING THEM ON
Once the feeder is cast into the water and
settles on the bottom, the river's currents will
push the bait out of the feeder, down stream
to where the fish are waiting.

ADDITIONAL EQUIPMENT

Swim feeders will be essential if
you're doing much river fishing, and
there are all manner of types and
designs. I would suggest a few open-
ended swim feeders, together with a
few closed swim feeders of various
weights. You might want to go as
light as ¾ of an ounce (20g) and up to
about 2½ ounces (70g) if you're
fishing a big river, or it's in flood.
Once again, a reputable brand is
important because swim feeders do
take an awful amount of bashing and
can break up.

Hooks are, of course, essential,
and I'd advise you to buy eyed hooks
with a wide selection between sizes 4
and about 18. The higher the
number, the smaller the hook – an 18
will be used for a maggot or two,
while the 4 can easily take a great
lump of bread or a couple of
lobworms. The numbers ascend in
twos, so in all you'll probably buy

around about 8 packets. Make sure
that you only buy the best. Like your
line, the hook is an absolutely critical
part of your tackle, and if it bends
open, the fish will be lost. Look for
hooks that are either barbless or
have micro-barbs: this will make
unhooking your first fish much
easier, and if that hook should get
into your own finger, then it will slip
out relatively painlessly.

You'll also need a box of split shot
– never use lead these days for fear
of harming wildfowl – some swivels
for attaching a hook length to your
main line, and, importantly, a pair of
forceps. These are invaluable tools
for unhooking a fish that has
swallowed a bait a little deeply.

You'll also need a landing net.
This is because it isn't a good idea to
swing any fish, let alone a big one,
straight onto the bank. Choose one
with a decent-sized frame and very
soft mesh, and do remember that you
don't always have to take a fish out
of the water once it's in the net. In
many instances, you can crouch
down over the net, unhook the fish,
and let it go straight back without
ever breaking surface. You might

want to buy a set of weighing scales.
However, I feel that many people
weigh too many fish without
thinking whether it's really
necessary or not. Weighing fish
simply increases the stress that
they're already experiencing.

You'll need a bag of some sort to
carry all this gear in; this is often
incorporated into a box if you feel
the need to sit down when you're at
the waterside. Alternatively, a small,
light stool will fit the bill.

TACKLE TIPS

1 You are fortunate if you live or
travel in the US. If not, do you have
a friend or relation going there?
Send for some catalogues, and mark
out the lures or other fishing
equipment that you want. You'll find
that everything is far cheaper there.

2 Look up before you tackle up! We
all know that carbon fibre, now the
most common rod material, is a
great conductor of electricity so
never fish within 100 foot (30m) of
an electric cable. Note that your rod
does not actually have to touch the
wires, as electricity can leap the gap.

3 Try to keep your reels in pouches
or put elastic bands over the spools
in your tackle bag. Nothing is worse
than a massive jumble of line that
seems to trap every piece of tackle.

4 After use, dry your rod on a soft
cloth or the damp will lift the epoxy
coating and destabilize the rings. In
the same way, do not store rods in
damp bags or sealed rod tubes.

5 If you keep your hooks in small
boxes, smear these with petroleum
jelly. This stops the hooks from
rusting. It also stops them moving
about and blunting their points.

6 If you are a regular fisher, you
should change your line at least
twice a year. Despite the UV
stabilizer now put into most lines,
they will deteriorate in sunlight.

◁ CAT'S WHISKERS
Monster catfish like this demand monster baits. This particular catfish was caught on a dead carp weighing about a pound. Always think very carefully about matching your quarry with the bait that it requires. Big baits for big fish is a golden rule.

◡ IN THE NET
Happiness is your capture netted! The next step is to place it back in the very shallow margins where it's easy to slip the hook out. You can then let the fish go, little the worse for its strange experience.

WHICH BAIT?

Now we come to the vexed question of bait – of which there are literally thousands of types. To start, let's try to simplify it as much as possible.

Firstly, there are the 'kitchen' variety of baits – bread, cheese, pepperami, luncheon meat, sweetcorn – almost anything you can find in the larder that will stay on a hook! In fact, bread, luncheon meat and sweetcorn will probably catch as many fish as most other types of bait.

Then there are shop-bought baits. For small fish on heavily pressured waters, maggots and their chrysalis, often called casters, are hard to beat. Virtually all good tackle dealers will sell these. Take care of your maggots, and don't let them overheat or run out of air, or you'll end up with a revolting gooey mess. Tackle dealers will also sell hemp seed, which works as a very effective ground bait once it's been boiled and allowed to simmer until the white insides show

through the black skin. A good deal of tackle dealers will sell this type of bait already prepared.

If it's pike you're after, you'll also need a few dead fish baits. You can use ordinary freshwater fish, but this

may pose problems for the local fish stocks. It's far better go to the fishmonger and buy mackerel, sardines or sprats. You can then take them to the water frozen as they will be much firmer to cast that way.

CARE OF BAIT

1 Don't let bread dry out in the sunshine or it will become too hard to mold around the hook. Try keeping it in a plastic bag in your pocket.

2 Keep both worms and maggots out of the heat or they'll soon die.

3 Keep worms moist, perhaps in moss or damp newspaper. If you notice a dead worm in the tin, remove it before it contaminates the rest.

4 Open cans of sweetcorn at home and pour the contents into a plastic bowl. Cans opened and discarded on the riverbank can be very harmful to wildlife, and to cattle in particular.

5 Dispose of unwanted bait thoughtfully at the end of the day. Nobody wants to see the banksides strewn with rotting sweetcorn and luncheon meat. Take home with you any food items that aren't easily going to be eaten by swans or wildfowl.

6 If you won't be fishing again for a while, tip away any unused worms or maggots on the river bank rather then leaving them to die in the bait tin.

7 Think about bait economy: for example, it's much cheaper to buy a large catering can of sweetcorn than it is to buy several small ones.

BAIT SELECTION

1 BREAD Use your loaf... sliced bread is a perfect hookbait.

2 SAUSAGE Cooked sausage can be cut into slices.

3 LUNCHEON MEAT This can be cut into any shape, and stays on the hook well.

4 CHEESE SPREAD Creates an excellent bait when mixed into a paste with bread.

5 CRUSTS Chunks of floating crust are especially good for carp.

6 SWEETCORN is an effective bait for most non-predatorial fish species.

7 FRUIT Even the humble banana will attract fish such as chub.

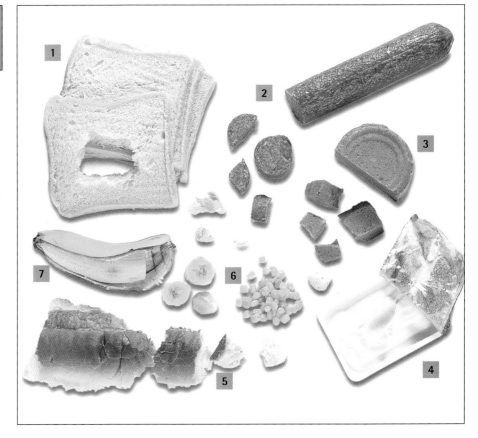

> THE SEARCHER
It always pays to look under big logs, stones or anything you find on the riverbank. You'll frequently find slugs, snails or worms – all of which are excellent natural baits that will tempt a wide variety of fish.

'BOILIES'

One of the greatest booms in the tackle industry has been the 'boilie' bait sensation. 'Boilies' are marble-like creations made out of eggs, a base mix such as soya, flavourings, and colourings. This mixture is then boiled till they form a hard outer skin. Boilies were developed originally for carp but they are now also used for barbel, tench, chub and bream. There are literally hundreds of different makes, and I would very much go with what the tackle dealer recommends if you think that boilies are essential.

Coming onto natural baits, worms dug from the back garden are devoured by almost every fish that swims. You can also try wading into the shallows of the river, turning over stones and collecting the grubs that you'll find hidden there. Caddis grubs are particularly good for most river species.

⋏ LIKE A HERON
Here I am wading the shallows looking for a big stone to turn over. All sorts of creatures colonize the bottom of our rivers and it's possible to find a whole range of natural baits there.

◁ CADDIS GRUBS
Just look at this rock that I've picked out. On it is a really juicy caddis grub that's made a little shelter for itself out of stones and sand. There it lives, secure from the outside world until it hatches into a fly. In its grub form, it's a perfect bait for all manner of fish.

LURE
FISHING

LURE FISHING

To catch a predatorial fish, you can either use a real fish – preferably dead – or an artificial one made out of wood, plastic, metal or rubber. The whole art of lure fishing is making inanimate objects look like a fleeing or wounded fish to any hungry predator and fooling the predator into thinking that he's up for an easy meal.

∨ SPINNER DELIGHT
This small but beautiful-looking perch was taken on a spinner in bright sunlight. It really does pay to experiment with different coloured blades according to varying light conditions.

There are times when you'll just have to use a real dead fish (see page 60). Perhaps the water is very cloudy or temperatures are particularly low – two conditions when predators prefer an easy meal that they can scoop up off the bottom. But for most of your predator fishing, lures are the most exciting, and one of the most efficient, ways of fishing. Lure

54

LURE FISHING EQUIPMENT

fishing has become more and more of an exact science over the last few years and there is now a bewildering array of shapes, sizes, colourings and designs on the market. Don't panic, though, take it simply at first, step by step, and the necessary know-how will gradually slip into place.

Although you can use almost any rod, you'll get more pleasure if you use something that is designed for the job. With lure fishing, you will be casting and retrieving all day long, so you don't want a rod that is too heavy. Nor do you want a rod that's too long – between 8 and 9 feet (2.4–2.7m) is ideal since this both cuts down on weight and increases casting accuracy. There are many lure rods on the market now, and many American models are available around the world, so no-one should have to pay top dollar.

1 SHOULDER BAG *When you're travelling light, this will carry all your gear.*

2 POLAROID GLASSES *These help you see the fish through the surface glare.*

3 FORCEPS *Forceps are necessary for removing hooks safely and easily.*

4 FIXED SPOOL REEL *A fixed spool reel is essential for trouble-free casting.*

5 TRACE WIRE *This is a must for all predators with sharp teeth.*

6 SPINNING ROD *Light and not too long, a good spinning rod should be comfortable and not too tiring on the arm.*

7 PLUG *A jointed plug gives out good vibrations as it wiggles through the water.*

8 METAL SPOON *A metal spoon has a good action in the water and catches the light. Note how both this and the plug are attached to a wire trace.*

9 TREBLE HOOKS *A selection of treble hooks for deadbaiting.*

10 WEIGHTS *Useful for taking a lure down deeper in the water, and for anchoring a deadbait on the bottom.*

11 PIKE FLOATS *A selection of pike floats in various sizes to suit different waters and deadbaits.*

12 THERMOMETER *The temperature of the water can be crucial. If it is very cold, then deadbaiting is likely to be more successful than a spoon or a plug.*

A THE LURE FISHER'S GEAR
A light, responsive reel with a delicate clutch mechanism is vital. Note that the rod in the photograph has a screw reel attachment for added security during constant casting.

Y LURE SUCCESS
This very fine pike – slightly off 30 pounds (13.5kg) – was landed on a mid-water plug worked around some big rocks in quite deep water. Pike will often use this kind of location as an ambush point. Try to think like a fish: if you see anywhere that could hide a big predator from passing prey fish, then it's worth investigating further.

CHOOSING YOUR EQUIPMENT

As for your reel, most will do providing that they're not too heavy. A relatively small fixed-spool reel – the one you probably use for float fishing on stillwaters or swim feeder fishing on rivers – will be ideal, providing it can take a 300 feet (90m) or so of 8 to 10 pound (3.6–4.5kg)

line. If you're using a light rod, remember you don't want to use too heavy a reel with it. The whole outfit just won't feel right, even to a beginner. If you really get into the game, then you might want to use one of the little multiplier reels that are so popular in the US. However, this is probably best kept till later.

Your line is particularly important in lure fishing as it takes a lot of battering. Remember, if you're ledgering say, you tend to cast out and leave your bait there for half an hour or even longer. When you're lure fishing, your line is working constantly, never at rest. That's why it always pays to buy a good, strong, resilient line. You might even think of trying braid. If you do go for a braid, which is an expensive but very tough, long-lasting option, do make sure you read the instructions on its packaging. The manufacturers may recommend a particular type of knot and it does pay to follow their advice.

You'll also need a wire trace, even if you're going for non-toothy predators such as perch or trout. The problem is that a pike, walleye or zander could just as easily take the spinner and cut ordinary line with their sharp teeth. This means that you lose a lure but, worse than that, you leave a fish with a lethal piece of ironmongery in its mouth. So, wire traces always, please!

You'll also need at least one swivel. Without a swivel you get tremendous twisting of the line and this can leave it kinked and useless within just a few minutes. Swivels do have a lot of constant work to do, so make sure that you buy a recognized make and not something too cheap that will let you down.

Your lure will be attached to the wire trace by means of a snap link. This is the last and most crucial piece of your armoury; if it twists and bends under pressure then you'll lose that fish. So, once again, the absolute advice is to ask your tackle dealer for a good, strong, reliable make that will never let you down.

These things may cost you a little more, but they are essential – not just for your own success rate, but also for the good of the fish.

LURE FISHER'S GLOSSARY

FORCEPS – forceps or pliers are very useful when it comes to getting the hooks out of the bony mouths of predators – especially pike. Often ones with quite long noses are very useful.

JIGGING – this is simply the act of moving a little spinner up and down through the layers of water to attract a predatory fish.

LURE – a general term given to an artificial creation meant to resemble a natural prey fish.

PLASTIC BAITS – small rubber lures meant to resemble such creatures as frogs, lizards, elvers and so on. They come in many different colours and look and feel fantastic.

PLUG – a plug is made out of wood, plastic, or metal and designed to look like a small prey fish. Some are built to work on the surface, some in mid water, and some down deep. Nearly all have a violent kicking action in the water that sends out vibrations.

SPINNER – a spinner is a small metal object that rotates through the water, catches the light, and looks like a small prey fish.

SPOON – a bigger piece of metal, made spoon-shaped so that it kicks and rotates through the water sending out signals to a hungry predator.

SWIVEL – the main line from the rod and reel is attached to a trace by a swivel. This lets the lure rotate without twisting the main line.

TRACE – a trace is the length of material – generally $1\frac{1}{4}$ feet (50cm) or so – that attaches the lure to the swivel at the end of the main line. This trace is generally made of wire – especially if pike, walleye, zander or muskies are expected. The teeth on these species can cut through ordinary nylon line.

TROLLING – trolling is always done from a boat. Anything from one to six rods is used and each has a plug, spinner or spoon attached to the end. The engine is fired up, the boat then sets off, and the lures are trolled around the water. This is a good method for big lake predators.

⋏ EASY DOES IT
It's at moments like this that things can go wrong. If the fish finds a final burst of energy, a last plunge or shake of the head can free a loose hook, so always be ready to give line instantly. Never try to net any fish until it is properly beaten and on its side. Try, if possible, to unhook every fish in the water.

◄ CLOSE-UP ON PLUGS
Plugs come in all sorts of shapes, sizes, and colours. Jointed plugs (the top and the bottom plugs shown here) often have a very dramatic wiggle indeed. When retrieved slowly they look just like a wounded fish – and an easy meal.

CHOOSING A LURE

Now, we get on to the lures themselves, and this is where it gets complicated. You'll face lots of decisions in your fishing life but one of the most important is choosing the right bait, either real or artificial, which will tempt the fish on the day. You've really got to try and put yourself in the position of the predator. What will it be looking for? What will it want to eat? How can you present an artificial lure to look like a real, living creature?

Remember that every little bit of imagination you put into retrieving your lure helps. You're there to make the thing look as real as possible.

Let's first look at plugs. A plug is simply a wooden or hard plastic lure designed to look and move exactly like a small prey fish. The advantage of plugs is that you can choose one for whichever depth of water you want to explore. There are all sorts of plug designs and you may find them bewildering at first. However, as a rough guide, it pays to buy a few

shallow divers that generally work from just under the surface, down to 6 feet (1.8m) or so. These plugs are ideal for weedy summer waters. Next, you'll probably buy a few top water plugs that work exactly where their name implies, right in the surface film, where they splutter and

▽ JIG-A-JIG
A typical selection of plastic lures, often called jigs. They look and feel like natural prey. The weighted head on the hook takes the rubber jig down to the bottom in a fluttering motion, and you twitch it back to the surface. Dynamite!

splash and really cause a commotion. The experience of drawing one of these back over the surface of the water, and watching the wake that it creates, can be very exciting… especially if an ever-growing bow wave is following it!

Then you'll need a few deep divers, which work at depths greater than 6 feet (1.8m) and can go down as far as 20 or even 30 feet (6–9m). These tend to be bigger lures, and they are mostly used in deep lakes throughout the northern hemisphere. They are especially useful in winter, or in very hot weather when fish go down deep to escape the sun.

With these three types of plug, you should have something in your box for most situations.

Soft plastic lures are made of rubberized plastic and come in all sorts of shapes and sizes. These are excellent for perch, trout, pike and zander. They are meant to imitate all kinds of underwater creatures… and some that have never existed at all. The soft plastic range includes worms, lizards, grubs, toads, frogs, rats, mice – just about anything you can think of that's ever swum across a pond. Some work on the surface, and some are intended to be jigged up and down closer to the bottom.

⋏ SLEEKLY SILVER
The zander – the closest of brothers to the American walleye – is a shoaling predator. It grows to around 20 pounds (9kg) maximum, but averages less than half that. This very beautiful fish was caught from the Caspian Sea on a small spinner. Deadbaits and small plugs work just as well.

Jigging is simple: you just keep a tight line to the lure and move your rod up and down, allowing it to rise and then fall with a fluttering type of motion. You'll find that perch, in particular, will take the lures as they go in either direction.

➤ BALTIC SUCCESS
This very fine Baltic pike was taken in the spring when it left the sea to come into one of the shallow bays to spawn. It's at this time of the year that huge gatherings of pike occur.

DEADBAITING

1 A deadbait, which the predator can detect by smell, can be highly effective when the weather is either very cold and/or the water is very cloudy. In cold, murky water, there's hardly any chance whatsoever of a pike, perch, zander, or whatever, actually seeing your lure, and in any case it probably wouldn't be inclined to expend valuable energy chasing it.

2 Never use wild fish for deadbait, but choose fish that were already destined for the table – small sea fish such as smelts or sardines, or small, farmed rainbow trout. If you stick to this type of bait, then you can be sure that you're not harming local stocks of wild fish.

3 Deadbaiting need not be boring. You can twitch deadbaits back through the water towards you – a method called sink and draw – or you can drift deadbaits under a float, which can be very exciting, especially when you see that float go down two hundred yards away.

4 Good bite indication is absolutely essential when you're fishing deadbaits. It's all too common for a pike or other predator to pick up a deadbait and munch it on the spot without moving your line more than an inch or two. The result of this is a deeply hooked fish, so keep your eye glued to your line or your float.

5 Barbless hooks, naturally, go along with the deadbaiting scene. If this makes casting long distances a problem, simply tie the bait to the trace wire with elastic bands to give added security. If you're using frozen dead sea fish as baits, hook them up frozen for a really long cast and they'll gradually thaw out in the water.

MORE LURES

Spoons are made of shaped sheet metal. When cast, their shape makes them wobble in the water. Their bright, shiny finish catches any sunlight and throws out tantalizing glints. Most spoons are rather heavy, and these are ideal for searching out deep, underwater features. It's essential when using spoons to have a good quality, strong swivel or you will find the line twists appallingly. Also, keep your spoon highly polished. The more it shines, the more effective it will be.

The final type of lure that we will concern ourselves with is the spinner. This has an angled blade with a propeller mounted on its shaft. When you retrieve a spinner, water resistance makes the blade rotate and flash, and this attracts all

LURE FISHING TIPS

1 Hook strips of fish or bacon rind onto the treble of a spinner – these can frequently tempt a wary fish.

2 Choosing the right spinner can be a nightmare, and it pays to buy a couple of each of the common patterns, try them out and build up your own experience.

3 Try working a surface lure at night, especially if the water is calm and there is a full moon. Fish tend to be very active during these periods, especially in the summer.

4 If you see a predator following your lure, do not under any circumstances slow down the retrieve. The lure will then look less than lifelike and the predator will lose interest. If anything, it pays to speed the lure up.

5 Try painting big white spots onto your large plug. These white spots will make the predator think that your artificial has a fungal disease and will be easy to catch.

6 Always carry a file with you when you're lure fishing. Just give those treble points an extra sharpening before fishing. This can make all the difference between a firmly hooked fish and one that shakes itself free.

7 Always flatten down the barbs on big trebles. If you don't, hook penetration can be difficult and unhooking an absolute nightmare.

8 Never forget to take a large, sturdy, pair of forceps with you when you go lure fishing. These are essential for unhooking any lure-caught fish. You simply cannot take the hooks out with your fingers – especially if the fish that you've just caught is a mean-looking pike.

9 If you don't live in the US and a friend is going there, send for some catalogues, mark out the lure fishing gear that you want and ask your friend to buy it for you. There is a wide range, and it is much cheaper.

types of predators. Size, colour and vibration are all important considerations when you're buying spinners but, again, don't worry – any decent tackle dealer will direct you to the well known brands that have been catching fish for generations. The most important thing is to have a few variations as sometimes a particular colour will work on a particular day when all else fails. My own favourites are silver and gold with a variety of spots – generally red – on the blade. I also find that red wool on the hook shank is another advantage, especially for fish species such as perch that will often follow a good few yards, pecking and nibbling, before making a final decision.

Make sure that you store your lures effectively. If you just throw them willy-nilly into any old box, you'll find that they tangle up together horrendously. There are many purpose-built lure boxes now on the market and my advice is to buy one. Don't forget your hook bonnets – these little plastic hoods fit over the treble hooks and ensure that they don't get tangled. They also make the lures safer for transit and for handling.

It pays to store your lures in a warm, dry environment. There's nothing worse than going to your lure box after a couple of months to find that the treble hooks, spinners, and spoons have all rusted in some damp shed.

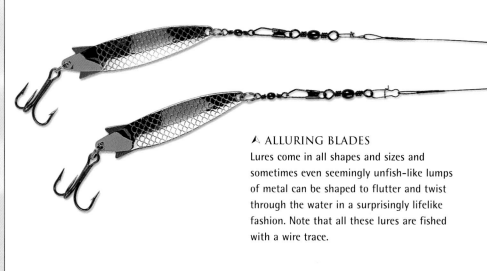

⋏ ALLURING BLADES
Lures come in all shapes and sizes and sometimes even seemingly unfish-like lumps of metal can be shaped to flutter and twist through the water in a surprisingly lifelike fashion. Note that all these lures are fished with a wire trace.

⋏ SPOON FED
The spinning spoon-shaped blades on these lures create flashes and vibration in the water, which attract predators in from a good distance. The flexible, flowing, rubber body is also reminiscent of a fleeing fish.

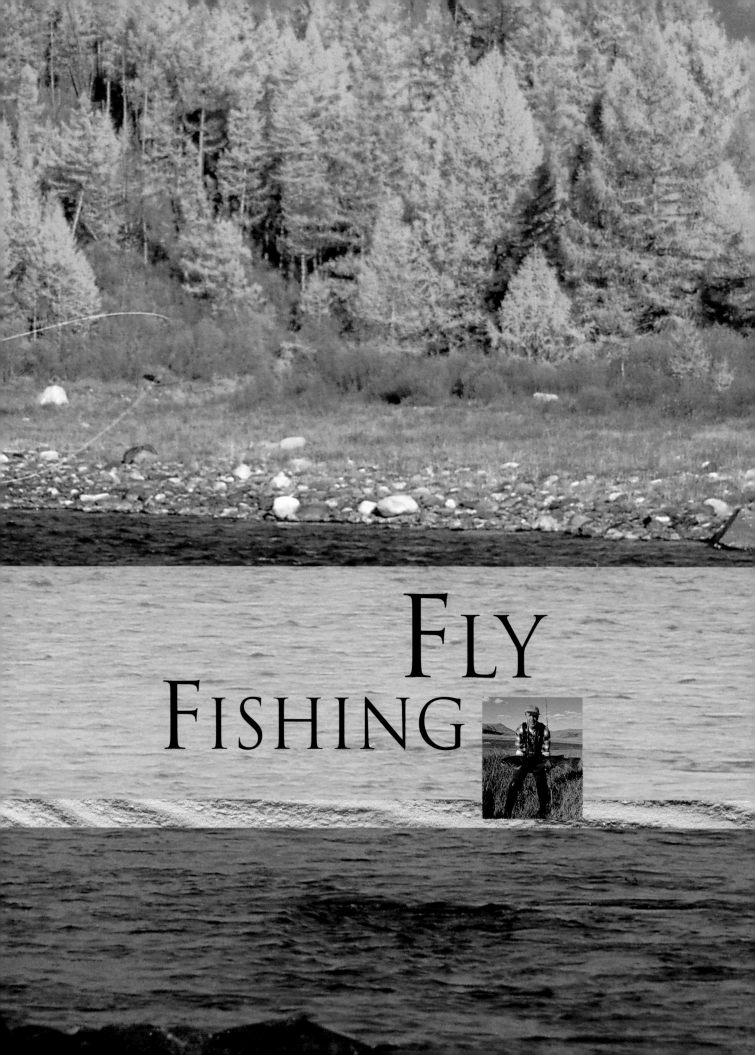

FLY FISHING

FLY FISHING

For hundreds, if not thousands of years, anglers have been trying to imitate insects with their own creations made of fur, feather or hair. The idea is to convince trout, grayling and salmon – commonly called gamefish – that the imitation is the real, living insect.

⋏ FIGHT ON

A big trout is hooked in a fast flowing river. Note how the rod is held up at an angle of about 45° or so, allowing its flexibility to cushion the lunges of the fish. See also how retrieved line is allowed to lie at the angler's feet. This is quicker than trying to get it back onto the reel.

Flies are obviously very light, so to cast them any distance from the bank you need weight. The weight is in the fly line itself, and a very flexible rod is capable of throwing this line many yards. Some of the flies float – these are the dry flies. Others sink – wet flies. Similarly,

some fly lines are designed to float and others to sink. If you want to get down deep to fish lying near the bottom, you can use a sinking line, but if you are using a dry fly, then you'll use a floating line.

Don't be too afraid about some of the exorbitant price tags you might

see on some rods, reels and lines in the tackle shop or catalogue. There's an enormous variety of tackle available in the fly-fishing world but believe me, you really can buy something at the bottom end of the market that is cheap but reliable and will serve you very happily for years.

FLY FISHING EQUIPMENT

1 HAT *A broad brim shades your face.*

2 POLAROID GLASSES *These let you see what flies the fish are taking.*

3 BAG *Useful for all your gear.*

4 PRIEST *Dispatches fish humanely.*

5 NYLON *Line in various strengths to make up your own casts.*

6 FLOATANT *Keeps dry flies afloat.*

7 BINOCULARS *Light binoculars can help you see what type of flies are hatching.*

8 FORCEPS *These are necessary to slip out the hook.*

9 LINE FLOATANT *Keeps line afloat.*

10 CASTS *Ready-made tapered casts are more expensive than home-made cast, but they are lovely to fish with.*

11 MULTI-TOOL *Has a host of uses.*

12 STRIKE INDICATORS *These are very useful if you are fishing nymph patterns.*

13 VARIOUS FLIES *The selection shown here includes wet flies, nymphs, dry flies and a large salmon fly.*

➤ A MOORLAND BEAUTY

Trout come in all shapes, forms and sizes and hugeness is no real indicator of quality. This very small but exceedingly beautiful trout came from a Scottish mountain stream at around 2000 feet (600m) altitude. Although the feeding is not particularly rich, the colouration is quite breathtaking.

FLY FISHER'S GLOSSARY

DRY FLY – an artificial fly that floats.

FLY LINE – a plastic or polymer-coated line that gives fly anglers the necessary weight to cast the fly out from the bank.

LEADER – this is a length of nylon line that attaches the heavy fly line to the artificial fly. It is tapered, thicker near the fly line and thinner toward the fly itself. The leader is generally about the length of the rod – longer in difficult situations.

LIE –a place where a trout decides to hang, particularly in a river.

NYMPHING – using an artificial that looks like a real nymph.

RISE – the name given to the act of a trout as it comes to the surface film and sips in an insect. The rise is also the name given to that period in the day when large numbers of trout come up to take insects.

SIGHT FISHING – this means stalking and casting to an individual fish that you have seen.

STRIKE – lifting the rod to set the hook once the fly has been taken.

TIPPET – the last yard or so of the cast leading toward the fly.

WET FLY – an artificial fly that sinks.

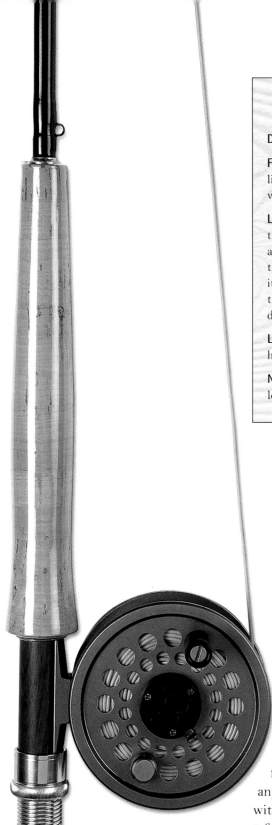

TACKLE FOR TROUT FISHING

My feeling is that you won't be starting with something as exotic as salmon, and that it's best to learn the trade on something more accessible. So let's look at rods, reels, lines, flies and accessories for the trout angler. The sort of rod to start off with is something round about 9 feet (2.7m) long that will carry any line weighted between No.6 and No.8. Rods and lines are given these figures so you know how to match them up. A No.1 weight, for example, is very light indeed for trout fishing on tiny little streams, whereas a No.10 outfit would be ideal for a big reservoir in very windy conditions. As I've already said, however, something between 6 and 8 is pretty well ideal for the beginner, and will suit virtually every condition.

Spending a lot is not necessary when choosing your first rod, although obviously the more you pay for your rod, the more sophisticated the product. Take the very best advice that you can find and, if at all possible, try the rod out for yourself. Many tackle dealers now have a pool behind their premises upon which you can have a few practice casts. This will enable you to make sure that you like the feel of your chosen rod and reel together. Harmony is the key word in fly fishing. Rod, reel and line should all be in balance, and you shouldn't feel that you are straining in any way.

➢ MONGOLIAN MONSTER
This, truly, is a fish to dream about. The mighty taimen is the oldest member of the salmon family and now has a range restricted to parts of Siberia, China and Mongolia. The fish can grow huge – to over a hundred pounds (45kg) – but they're still catchable on the fly if you're prepared for a mighty battle.

ᐱ FLY TACKLE
A brand new fly rod and reel almost ready to go. I say almost, because the shiny cellophane wrapping has yet to be taken off the cork handle or it will sweat and distort once it is in use and gets damp. Note the screw fitting for the reel. This is to grip it tightly to the rod during the exertions of casting.

FLY FISHING LINES

Many would say that the reel for the fly fisherman is only a storage mechanism. To some degree this is quite true, unless you hook a very big fish that begins to take off lots of line and then you've got to think about gearing drags and all things technical! However, to get started, simply choose a cheap reliable reel that will hold your line and plenty of backing. Above all, ensure that the reel seems to fit snugly with the rod. If the outfit doesn't feel in balance, then try some other combination. Try to find a product that offers one or two spare spools with your reel – this will allow you to change fly lines if you feel the need.

Fly lines can appear to be a minefield for the beginner, and indeed there are many companies offering countless different designs. Don't panic. To start with, you'll probably just need a floating line and a medium sinking line in case you want to get your fly a little bit deeper. There are many other types – some that sink like stones, for example – but these are really designed for specialist work and you're best starting off with the two I've already mentioned.

Lines also come in various different profiles, and the most common are double taper or those with weight-forward designs. In fact, the weight-forward line is now dominating the market, and I'd probably advise you to go for one in the first instance. Weight-forward simply means that there is a heavier

▲ THE END OF THE RAINBOW
This beautiful rainbow trout was taken from a high altitude stream in British Columbia. Like all trout species, rainbows can differ from one watershed to the next but what all rainbow families share is a willingness to go for the fly, both on the surface and beneath. They also have a real gameness when it comes to the fight. This particular fish jumped at least eight times.

➤ STEELHEAD GLORY
Steelheads are just rainbow trout that go to sea for much of their lives rather than staying in freshwater all the time. The steelheads then come back to freshwater to spawn, and this is when anglers can catch them on the fly. They are truly mighty fish, possibly the hardest fighting game fish you'll ever hook.

'head' to the line, which helps shoot it out when you're casting. Don't go for one of the extreme examples – this again is for specialized work. Colour is also a consideration; something visible but not too glaring is my tip – you could do worse, perhaps, than a light green.

I've been emphasizing that price is not a major consideration with rods and reels, but when it comes to line I would push the boat out as far as you can. It's often a false economy to go for the cheapest – cheap line tends to break up quickly and never makes casting particularly easy.

You'll be attaching a nylon leader onto your fly line. As you get more experienced, you can make these up yourself. However, when you first start, it's useful to buy a few tapered ones straight from a reliable manufacturer. This will help your casting no end in the beginning, and help avoid all manner of frustrations.

⋏ DAWN WONDERLAND
Dawn is one of the most productive times for fly fishing for certain species. Salmon often move in the half-light before they settle down into a deep hole to see out the day. Grayling, too, are often very active, and sometimes you'll find that odd big trout vulnerable early in the day. Look for the shallows where fish hunt overnight, and present a biggish fly in the tiny pools formed here and there by rocks.

CHOOSING THE RIGHT FLY

1 It's always advisable to buy the very best flies available – after all, they are the most crucial part of the trout fisher's armoury.

2 It's hard to tell a good fly simply by looking, so in the first instance, go for a proven brand or tier.

3 Make sure the tying of each fly looks neat, with no loose ends. Durability is very important, and you don't want something coming apart after two or three casts.

4 If you are buying a nymph, make sure that it looks slim and stream-lined. It is very important how a fly behaves in the water – you need it to act as much like the insect it is imitating as possible.

5 It's also important to consider the hook type. Buy flies that are tied to hooks that have a good reputation. The last thing you want is a hook gape to straighten out when your first or best brown trout is sliding towards the net.

6 It's always a good idea to buy at least two flies of each pattern you choose. There's nothing more annoying than losing the 'taking' fly of the day in a tree, and finding that you have no replacement in the box.

⋏ FOOLED

A small nymph-like fly pattern has accounted for this fine grayling. Although the fly may look insignificant, it imitates very convincingly the small aquatic insects that grayling and trout both feed on. Grayling will often accept such an offering just drifted down in the current.

⋏ THE STRIKE INDICATOR

Grayling will accept a nymph drifting with the current, but they take it at lightning speed and it's all too easy to miss the event altogether. This is where the strike indicator comes in – a small piece of plastic, polystyrene or whatever is placed up the line so that the nymph floats beneath it at the required depth. Once a grayling sucks it in, the mini-float dives, you strike, and the battle is on.

OTHER USEFUL ACCESSORIES

Before we get on to the tangled question of fly choice, there are one or two other things on the market that you'll find helpful.

A product such as Permaflote is useful if you want to make a dry fly or leader float. There are also products that will help to make your leader sink well. Alternatively, soak a piece of sponge in washing-up liquid – you'll find this does the job nearly as well when the leader is pulled back through it.

Strike indicators are pieces of plastic that stick on the leader, show up brightly and act in the same way as a fisherman's float. Choose ones that are light, highly visible and stick to the leader during casting. You will find these very useful if you are fishing for grayling in the winter, for example, or using nymphs for trout down deep. (Do watch out though and check local rules – they are frowned upon on some waters.)

You'll certainly need a fly box.

Once again, there are plenty on the market, with many at budget prices. There's no great advantage going for something really fancy early on.

You will also need clippers to finish off your knots, and a hook sharpener is a very good idea, especially when the trout are rising in a finicky mood.

On many waters, you will be able to take home the trout that you catch, so you will need a priest (see page 65) to tap a fish on the head. Do not, under any circumstances, try to kill a fish without a priest. Rummaging around on the bank for a stick or a stone while a fish is flipping its life away miserably is not a humane way to act.

➢ ON TOP OF THE WORLD

What a feeling – this young angler is surveying the awesome, endless beauty of Greenland. Often, you have to be prepared to walk good distances in remote areas to get the very best fishing, so it pays to travel light. Rod, reel, flies, food and liquid, and off you go... taking care to tell those in the camp your exact route.

LURES, NYMPHS AND DRY FLIES

Finally, of course, you'll need some flies. Go into any serious tackle dealer and you will be overwhelmed by the choice. Again, don't panic. There are simple rules to follow.

Let's start with lures first – largish flies, tied to imitate small fish, or anything to attract a trout's curiosity. You should carry a stock of lures in the principle colours of black, white, yellow and orange. Stock up on some leaded and some unleaded, with a selection of different sizes. There are days when a lure will work exceptionally well for no apparent reason, so it pays to experiment with what you've got until you find the right fly.

All anglers should then aim to build up a selection of at least the popular, well-tried, nymphs. Once more, these should vary in size and colour, with some leaded and some unleaded. Remember that there are some trout experts who fish nearly all their lives with hardly anything but nymphs. Start off with tried and tested favourites such as the Pheasant Tail and perhaps some of the Czech-type nymphs that imitate caddis grubs and shrimps.

A dry fly is one that floats on the surface – the most obvious example being the huge and beautiful mayfly. Anyone fishing streams, and even stillwaters, in the early summer should have a few mayflies in the box. Beyond that, ask the advice of the tackle dealer about favourites on your local waters, and build up a small selection that should be able to match the hatch reasonably closely at any given moment.

◄ END OF THE DAY
Sometimes it is justified to take a very fine trout like this for the table. Here, Joy and I were camping at least 50 miles away from the nearest settlement and it was important that we caught our own food to survive.

A FLY FISHER'S SELECTION

1 STREAMER FLY *A large streamer fly is useful for big trout, steelhead pike, anything that wants a large meal.*

2 RESERVOIR LURE *A reservoir lure such as this is excellent for rainbow trout.*

3 WET FLIES *Traditional wet flies are best fished on quick rivers for trout and grayling.*

4 SALMON FLY *An good example of a fly that will attract salmon.*

5 DRY FLIES *These are perfect for the summer and autumn trout river.*

6 NYMPHS *Nymphs are the standard patterns for deeper feeding trout and grayling.*

⌄ WHERE TO BEGIN

You arrive at a large water like this early in the morning and wonder where on earth to begin. Look for any rising fish. See if there's any wind pushing the surface and try to fish close to the ripple. Look for overhanging trees or an island within casting range. Look for any shallows or any bays. Take your time, don't rush.

WET FLIES AND GOLD HEADS

It would be a mistake to ignore the traditional wet flies that grayling and trout anglers have used for centuries, especially if you're thinking of fishing any of the rougher streams. These are gaudy, colourful flies that are not really tied to represent any food item in particular. They just give a general impression of something edible; a Bloody Butcher is typical. Go for a small selection of different sized wet flies that feature reds, blues, greens and blacks, perhaps with an odd dash of silver here and there. It's probably true to say that the actual choice of wet fly is not generally too critical – it's how you fish it that's important. But more of that later.

Next on the shopping list come gold heads, which are really just nymphs, but with a golden bead tied to the top for weight and for 'flash'. Once again, buy a small selection of different sizes and different colours. My own favourites tend to be tied in red, orange and sometimes black.

Finally, no angler's fly box is complete without just a few buzzers, tied to represent midges that hatch out of the surface film, particularly

⋏ YOUR FIRST TROUT
Although most trout worldwide are now unhooked in the water and slipped back, your first trout is always something special and, of course, all trout are very good to eat. This particular fish was caught on a snail-like imitation just under the surface.

⋞ A MAGICIAN AT WORK
Fly tying can look a magical occupation, fit only for wizards, but it's an artform that we can all learn. Tying your own flies is cheaper than buying shop-bought patterns and immensely satisfying. In fact, many people like tying flies more than they do fishing them!

in the evening. Buzzers are generally quite small; red, orange and black are favoured colours.

Building up a fly collection will take time. My tip is to buy half a dozen or so each time you go into the tackle shop. That way, it's not too heavy on the pocket. Bear in mind that you're going to lose some, especially when you start, and you may feel that every tree and every reed is out to spite you!

Look after your flies. Don't let damp get into your fly box, or you'll find that all the hooks will rust quickly. If you do have a spillage, take the box out of your bag at home and dry it out thoroughly next to a radiator.

Finally, you'll probably need a light bag to hold all this gear as you wander the riverbanks. Alternatively, you can probably get away with a fly fisherman's waistcoat, which features a whole warren of pockets capacious enough to swallow fly boxes, extra reel spools, priests, even the odd bottle of beer! The choice is yours, but for me, as I like to travel as light as possible, I'd go with the vest.

⅄ THE CZECH NYMPH STYLE
In Central Europe, anglers have developed a very effective style of fishing nymphs. They wade very close to the fish, fish the nymphs deep along the bottom, and maintain constant contact. As soon as that line stops or tightens, a strike is made and the fish is on.

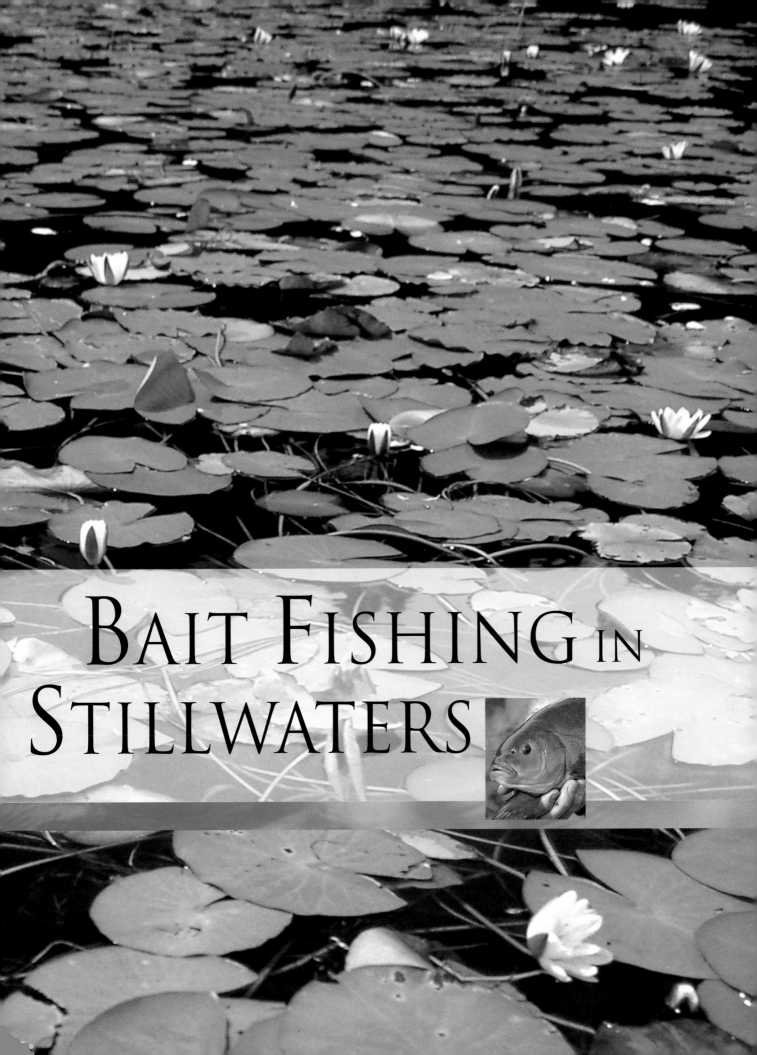

BAIT FISHING IN STILLWATERS

BAIT FISHING IN STILLWATERS

A LARGE STILLWATER CAN BE A VERY DAUNTING PROPOSITION WHEN YOU ARE STILL A RELATIVELY INEXPERIENCED ANGLER AND NEW TO THE WATER. THERE ARE NO FISH IN SIGHT, AND THERE MAY BE NO OBVIOUS FEATURES THAT MIGHT CAUSE THEM TO CONGREGATE. WHERE ON EARTH DO YOU BEGIN?

A good way is to ask advice, perhaps from somebody who knows a water better than you do, probably from the bailiff. Bailiffs always want to see anglers succeed – their living depends on the sale of tickets and a successful fisherman is one who will return to a particular water.

Failing this, there are several major factors to consider. Firstly, where is the wind coming from? Many, if not most, types of freshwater species tend to follow the wind, gradually moving toward the bank that it's hitting. In Europe, we are generally faced with westerly winds, and this tends to mean that the easterly shores are a good place to start.

Equally important is the question of cover. Smaller prey fish will never stray far from the refuge of reed and weed beds. A lot of fish also like to escape from the hubbub, so if there's a large, busy car park, then consider

⌃ HERE FOR THE DAY
Many stillwater bait fishermen settle on one swim – a piece of water – for the whole day, and try to attract fish into it by feeding in bait, gradually and persistently. They will set up several different rods so that they can fish close in or far out as conditions and the movements of the fish dictate.

⌃ THE WINTER LAKE
Winter fishing can be particularly difficult, as the cold weather makes the fish slow down and move less. This means location is crucially important. Try fishing close to dying reed beds or the remains of weeds that you can see just under the surface. If you can find them, also try deeper depressions in the lake's bed.

Location is probably the most vital consideration when fishing on large stillwaters. Fortunately, there are some real strong pointers to help you choose the best place to begin your fishing.

1 Dams. The dam wall of a reservoir or estate lake, for example, is always a good starting-off point. Fish like the depth that the dam wall offers and there's often a lot of food amongst the stone work.

2 Never ignore weed, reed and lily beds.

3 Islands attract fish, especially when they are overhung by trees or heavy reed growth.

4 Inflows. Many fish congregate where a stream runs into a stillwater, hoping to profit from food being washed down. This is especially significant after rain, when the incoming stream might also help colour up the lake and make fish feed with greater confidence.

5 Springs frequently bubble up to the surface of a lake or pool. These can be very attractive to fish in hot weather conditions when the water gets very stale and begins to lack oxygen.

6 Deep central channels often run down the middle of estate lakes. These are frequently the old streambeds that were dammed hundreds of years ago to make the lake in the first place. Fish will often congregate in this deeper water because of security and because of rich feeding. Look especially in these areas for tench, bream and carp.

7 Boathouses are frequently home to large perch shoals. The perch like to rub themselves against the submerged timbers and they also enjoy the shade from sunlight.

taking a good long walk with your binoculars to see what the more remote areas of the lake can offer. Bream and tench in particular will often move as far away as possible from commotion, and the angler who is prepared to use his legs starts off at a great advantage.

What other strategies can you follow? Look at lily pads, a very common feature on many stillwaters. These pads have magnetic qualities for carp and perch in particular. However, you will have to remember that stronger than average gear is

A HOT SPOT
There are certain clues every experienced bait fisherman looks for. Seek out those areas where surface scum has built up during the course of the day. All sorts of insect and food are trapped here and the fish won't be far away.

needed when you're fishing around the pads because the lily stems can be very tough indeed. Don't compromise on this, it's not fair on the fish if you lose it, leaving a hook in the mouth. Dribble in a few pieces of floating bait – bread crust or dog mixer biscuits are both ideal – and sit back quietly to see what happens. Watch for subtle movements amidst the pads. Then, perhaps, you will see the lips of the fish as it gently pulls the bait down. Carp are very likely to be responsible, but rudd and even crucian carp will also scan the surface film. Once you see activity like this, simply flick out a hooked bait and watch for the line slithering off.

A PERFECT DAY
The weather is cloudy and mild, and a brisk wind is blowing from the west. Fish will feed all through the day, especially if they're close to a structure such as an island, which gives them extra confidence.

◄ IT'S A LONG STORY

This carp, believe it or not, pulled an angler's rod off the bank and into the lake. James, the water keeper, got into a canoe and retrieved the tackle with the fish still on it. Message: never leave tackle unattended.

▲ THE CUNNING CRUCIAN

Crucian carp are as clever as anything that swims. Look for them very close to the bank, often under overhanging trees or right in the roots themselves. Bites are very cautious, so strike if your float moves the merest whisker.

USING SUB-SURFACE BAIT

A sub-surface bait can also work well, especially if it's a natural one. Remember that the fish are in the pads not just for protection, they are also looking for food – snails are particularly fond of lily pads and provide a good mouthful for a carp. Try using a small float and, perhaps, a couple of lively redworms fished about 18 inches (45cm) under the surface. Perch and carp often find this approach irresistible.

Whatever you hook in the pads, try to get them out into the open water as quickly as possible. Upon being hooked, many fish can be puzzled for just a few seconds and this gives you a chance to bully them clear. If a fish gets deep down amongst the roots of the lilies then you are in real trouble – you've got to set about the fight with real confidence in your tackle.

REED BEDS AND TENCH

Let's now look at reed beds, and at tench, the species that really adores them. Probably the most sought after type of reed are bulrushes. This is because bulrushes like to grow on a hard, clean, gravely bed – exactly the sort of place that tench prefer to feed. Bait up carefully with a mixture of sweetcorn, hemp seed, casters and a few maggots. Try to put the groundbait and your own tackle as close into the bulrushes as you possibly can. This is because the tench will often be swimming and feeding deep in the watery jungle. Laying-on is a super method for tench, very traditional, but none-theless effective. This involves applying sufficient split shot to the line to keep the bait on the bottom and the float "cocked," or upright. Tench will often pick the bait up, causing the float to rise or fall flat – so pay attention!

Look out for tench bubbles too, clusters of tiny, pinprick type bubbles that explode and fizz on the surface. Sometimes bits of bottom debris will also float to the surface, a sign that a group of fish is really rooting around and feeding hard… hopefully on your groundbait.

ʌ WITCH'S CAULDRON
When fish really get their heads down and begin to feed on the bottom, they can send up very impressive arrays of bubbles. What you hope is that they're feeding on your bait and not natural foodstuffs.

ʏ OLD RED EYE
The red eye of the tench is the trademark of this very careful fish. Look for it on the bottom where it feeds on bread, worms or maggots. Bites are hesitant, and can take half a minute to develop. Don't strike at the first indications.

VARYING YOUR BAIT

If you're not getting bites, then ring the changes with your hook baits. Try three grains of corn on a size 10 hook, or one grain on a size 16. Try two maggots and one caster on a size 12 hook, or two casters and a grain of corn on a size 10. Sooner or later you're more than likely to come across a winning combination.

Bream are a species that quite frequently likes to hang out a long way from the bank, and this means it's often necessary to approach them with long casting. First of all try, if at all possible, to locate your shoal.

⋏ STARTING OUT

There's always the problem of where to begin. It's never a bad idea to actually look for fish, especially if the day is bright, the water is clear, and you've got Polaroid glasses. Failing that, look for areas with cover, the sort of places that give fish confidence. Deep holes are often attractive during daylight hours.

⋏ TAKE YOUR TIME

Never be in too great a hurry to start. Take time out to sit and watch the water and build up a picture of what's going on. Look for any fish that rolls. Look for bubbles breaking the surface. The water is like a map, lying there giving you all sorts of directions towards destination success!

Either put in a few, large balls of groundbait and wait for the swim to settle, or feed smaller amounts more frequently that cause less tumult. Generally, the latter plan is the best – only use the former if you've got plenty of time.

▼ THE CHEF AT WORK
Preparing groundbait calls for imagination. Hemp seed, breadcrumb, sweetcorn and maggots are all obvious favourites, but don't overlook anything else that seems appealing. Never be afraid to experiment.

Look carefully at the water in front of you and see if you can spot any flat areas in patches of rippled water. This could well be a fish moving heavily just under the surface. Or, most excitingly, look for bream actually breaking the surface in a head and shoulders, slow, porpoise-like roll. Alternatively, you'll sometimes just see the tips of black fins, or perhaps a big area of coloured water, which means the bed is being disturbed by feeding fish.

Once you've found fish, you'll probably need to put out some light groundbait to get them feeding. Perhaps they're close enough for you to do this by catapult. If they are, mix your groundbait very stiffly and fire out small balls, just a little away from the fish. Whatever you do, don't put big balls on top of them as you will scare them. Mix maggots and casters into the groundbait.

▲ DAWN GLORY

If at all possible, always try to get to your lake before sunrise, because this is one of the times when all fish feed at their hardest. You might find a mist rising and the water surface like a mirror, but the fish will be active everywhere... bubbles, fish rising or even jumping. It's an exciting time to be out.

USING A SWIM FEEDER

If the fish are too far away for this, then you could try using a swim feeder on line of about 4 pounds (1.8kg) breaking strain.

Vary your hook length – start off at approximately 2 feet (60cm), though sometimes it's wise to go much longer than this. Your hook length can also be very slightly lighter – try 3 or 4 pound (1.3–1.8kg) breaking strength perhaps. A small hook, say a 16, and a couple of maggots are a good starting-off point for average sized bream in the 4 to 6 pound (1.8–2.7kg) category. No luck? Then try a pinch of breadflake, a small brandling worm

⅄ THE SWIM FEEDER

Swim feeders like this one are ideal for getting both the hook bait and free samples of bait out at a distance. With a feeder like this, you can cast far further than when using a float. Make sure that your reel has plenty of line on the spool and stop the swim feeder with a swivel. Begin with a hook length of around about 18–24 inches (45–60cm) for most conditions.

or any cocktail of maggots, worms and sweetcorn. Just as when you're tench fishing, keep an open mind and keep on experimenting.

For bite indication, you can either use a quiver tip or a butt indicator.

Don't be in too great a hurry to strike – some expert bream handlers advocate sitting on your hands till the reel handle begins to turn! This is to prevent you pulling the bait out of the bream's mouth, and they often

do take quite a time before they pass it beyond their lips. Try to bully a hooked bream away from its fellows as soon as you can, or the fish will plough through the shoal, causing great alarm as it does so.

TACKLE TIPS

1 Although lakes and reservoirs are called stillwaters, they are very rarely without movement generated by the wind. This can prove very annoying, because your line will begin to bow, pulling your float under and making striking difficult if you're fishing with a swim feeder at range. If you're float fishing, it's a good idea to put a very small shot about 12 inches (30cm) up the line from the float. This sinks the line and helps to stop drift. If you're ledgering, sink the rod tip after you've cast out, and wind in until everything is tight. The line should remain sunk and out of the main drift. You can also soak your line in washing-up liquid, which takes the grease off and makes it sink faster.

2 When fishing shallow, clear, water on a sunny day, try blackening the last

few yards of line with a waterproof black marker pen. This dulls the glint of the nylon and can result in you getting many more bites.

3 Fish can sometimes be suspicious of a heavy hook that keeps bait bedded on the bottom. If they suck at a bait and the weight of the hook doesn't let it rise, then they'll ignore it altogether. Try, therefore, a floating caster or two on the hook to give the bait a little buoyancy. If you're very cunning, it's a good idea to put some maggots in an ⅛ of an inch (3mm) of water for half an hour with the lid on the box. You will find they absorb the water and float. This means that the hook weight is neutralized, and is much more easily sucked into the mouth of a feeding fish.

4 When you are catapulting groundbait out, go for a low flight path in a wind, as it is less likely to be blown off course.

5 When ledgering, it can pay to tug the line between the reel and the bottom ring occasionally. A bait that moves from time to time can trigger an instant bite.

6 Paint some of your quiver tips white with a bottle of liquid paper. This will make them show up much better at dusk, dawn and at night in a torch beam.

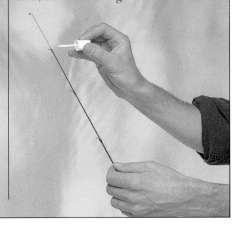

BAIT FISHING
IN RIVERS

BAIT FISHING IN RIVERS

N AN IDEAL WORLD, YOU'D WANT TO START FISHING WHERE YOU CAN ACTUALLY SEE DECENT FISH OF THE SORT YOU WANT TO CATCH. HOWEVER, LET'S PRESUME THIS ISN'T THE CASE, SO WHERE ON EARTH DO YOU BEGIN?

⅄ GLORY IN THE AUTUMN
Grayling really come into their own once the autumn frosts begin. Fish for them with a moving bait under a float like this one. Maggots and small redworms are excellent grayling baits, but beware – they give very quick bites.

The major factors to consider when reading a river are the strength and direction of the current, the depth, the amount of cover and the make-up of the riverbed. Most species of fish like to hang where the current is neither too strong nor too slow, where there's a fair amount of water to cover their backs, where they can find shelter from predators, and where there is clean gravel or sand over which they can find food easily.

Once again, though, let's look at some typical river hotspots and discuss some of the best approaches to fish them. Above all, anglers – and fish, fortunately – are attracted to mill pools or weir pools where foaming, well-oxygenated, water

tumbles over the sill. There's no doubt that fish welcome this freshening of their environment, especially in summer. And when you have low, hot conditions, you will find big populations amassing.

But how do you fish a mill pool? There are various areas to concentrate on: try right in the quick, foaming, white water for roach, chub or barbel. Where the current steadies up a bit, but there is still a lot of depth, is an ideal haunt for bream. As the mill pool shallows and glides into its traditional riverbed, it produces streamy, gravely water, often with abundant weed – perfect once again for barbel and chub.

⅄ TOP SPOTS
A weir like this is a magnet to many fish species. The falling water oxygenates the river beneath, and the action of the quick water also tends to dislodge the aquatic insects that the fish are looking to feed upon.

READING THE RIVER

1 Bridges always prove a magnet for fish, especially the deep pools that form down stream.

2 Fallen trees offer fish shelter from the current and protection from predators.

3 Big underwater rocks always attract bottom feeders.

4 All fish adore overhanging trees.

5 Deep pools will always hold fish in the winter and during summer droughts.

6 Bends are the favourite areas for prey fish and predators alike.

7 In places, the river will narrow and deepen. This is a perfect place for all river species.

◄ OLD RUBBER LIPS
A chub might have a big mouth and a big appetite to go with it, but it is in actual fact one of the most cunning of all fish species. They have big eyes and they can see exactly what is going on both in and above the water. The message is clear: approach them very carefully and offer them a really juicy bait perfectly presented. And don't make a splashy cast – you won't get another chance.

FOAMING WATER CONDITIONS

Let's look in greater detail at the foaming water under the mill itself: it will be deep there, anything up to 10 or 15 feet (3–4.5m), or even more on a large river. Try fishing tight under your rod tip with a float and a big lump of breadflake on the bottom. The current will move your tackle around every now and again, lifting the bait up and nudging it over the bottom stones and brickwork. This proves irresistible for both roach and chub, so expect bites to be quite ferocious. As for ground bait, dunk two or three slices of bread in the water and once they're thoroughly

⩒ READING THE WATER

In this water, there are areas of shallow gravels with quick current and other areas where the water deepens and slows. As a general rule, try the shallows both early and late in the day and go for the deeper water when the sun is up.

⩓ KEEPING IT DOWN

A flat lead like this holds the bottom very well in a very quick current. If you want to move your bait around, try a bullet lead that bounces more easily. It's useful to keep your bait in a bucket that you can fix to a belt.

BEST RIVER CONDITIONS

1 Most fish feed best just on the point of dusk and an hour into darkness. Dawn is also a good time.

2 If it rains heavily, and the river begins to rise and colour, you will find that barbel come furiously on the feed.

3 After heavy rain, the river begins to drop and the colour very slowly goes out of it – excellent conditions for all fish.

4 When the weather has been mild for a few days in the winter, with winds from the west, roach, barbel and chub will all feed hard.

5 A thunderstorm can pep-up a stale uncooperative river during a hot summer period.

◄ TO CATCH A CHUB

The rig could hardly be simpler – a largish hook (perhaps a size 4) baited with bread, and a single SSG shot, or even a couple of smaller shot if the water is slower moving and you have more time to sink the bait.

▼ JOB NEARLY DONE

Fishing is often about team work, and it makes sense to get somebody to net a big fish for you if you're at all unsure. Don't feel shy about asking. If you are netting a fish, keep the net in the water and draw the fish over it.

wet, mash them up and dribble them in around your float so you have a curtain of falling crumbs.

Rafts are always magnetic for chub, and for barbel to only a slightly lesser degree. A raft is simply all the drifting weed, leaves and rubbish that builds up when it catches against the overhanging branches of a tree. Soon the rafts can have the surface area of a fair-sized rug and the fish love the shelter on offer. The strategy here is to sit a good 5, or even 10, yards (4.5–9m) upstream and just flick in thumbnail-sized pieces of squeezed bread over a period of half an hour or so. Feed in perhaps 30 or even 40 pieces; a couple every minute is fine. The purpose behind this is to allay any suspicions the chub may have of the hook bait.

Now you're ready to fish: a size 4 hook with a big piece of bread squeezed around the shank is all you need. Place an SSG shot about 6 inches (15cm) up from it, 2 (5cm) if the current is quick. Simply flick the bread a yard (1m) or so upstream of the raft and let it sink down underneath. Prepare for an almost instant bite. You can hold the line round your fingers and feel for that rat-tat tug. Strike and then bully the fish hard from the tree roots, return it upstream and then try again in half an hour or so and you will probably be rewarded with another fish or two.

FISHING THE CREASE

Bends nearly always attract fish, especially on typical lowland rivers that have been dredged in the past and offer few features. They're also very attractive in the winter, especially when the river is in flood. Look for what anglers call the crease – that's where the current is separated from the slack water that all bends produce. You'll actually see where the fast and slow water meet – there is a real dividing line. This is the crease where chub and roach especially love to hang. Here, they can move in and out of the current, sometimes intercepting food, sometimes deciding to rest. One of the best methods of fishing is a very light ledger. Alternatively, and much more enjoyable, is to float fish using a decent-sized stick float that trundles a bait around the bottom, just a little bit slower than the river is moving. Once again, bread is a good bait, this time pinched on a smaller hook, say a size 10. A bunch of two or three maggots also works well. Dribble in loose feed – a few pieces of bread, say, every five minutes or so, or a dozen or so maggots every cast. Bites are very distinct.

ᴧ TROTTING RIG
A fairly large-bodied float has been set up with a shotted line and a piece of sausage – a bait that stays on the hook well.

ᴠ AT ONE WITH THE RIVER
This angler has waded way out into the river so he can fish a deep run under a tree on the far bank. He wants to fish with a float because he knows he can move a bait very naturally, and he's expecting quick, decisive bites.

FREE LINING

There are likely to be long, fast-flowing stretches on your river, full of broken water and gurgling rapids. The depth will be 2 or 3 feet (60–90cm). You will find this a perfect place for chub or barbel, especially in the early summer. Here you can try free lining, one of the most exciting ways of fishing. All you need, literally, is a hook on the end of your line and a decent-sized bait to give a bit of weight. Two lobworms are ideal, or even a small dead fish such as a gudgeon. Try to wade out from the bank – always making sure it's safe of course, and, ideally, that you've got a friend to offer help if there's a problem. Then, once you've got a secure footing, simply flick the

bait out into the flow, open the bail arm of the reel, and pay out line as the current drags the worms along. Keep tight to the bait, keep pulling your rod up until you can feel its weight. If you give slack, a fish can take the bait without you having a clue. Bites tend to be long pulls after a sudden build-up of pressure. Strike hard because sometimes the current will have taken your bait 50 or more yards (45m) down river. Then prepare yourself for a massive battle!

➤ LEDGERING A BAIT
A small weight, or ledger, attached to the line with a link will keep your bait on the bottom. When a fish takes the bait, the line pulls freely through the link, so it feels no resistance until you strike.

⩓ A LOVING RETURN
This barbel was caught on sweetcorn with a swim feeder. The bite was savage and the battle even more so. The angler has unhooked it and is returning it without ever needing to take it onto the bank.

◄ TOUCH LEDGERING IN ACTION
This is an exciting way to fish, as you wait for a tug on the line. Note how the line is held over the index finger, possibly the most sensitive of all the fingers. The messages you receive down the line are many and varied. Hold the rod around the reel handle and you'll find everything is well-balanced and you won't get tired through the course of the day.

TACKLE TIPS

1 Make sure that you always have a white quiver tip with you: it is very much easier to see than a red one, especially in poor light.

2 If you're not getting bites, look very carefully at your hook length. Sometimes, if you have a long hook length and the current is fast, the bait will lift from the bottom and revolve slowly in the flow of water, looking very unnatural. If this is the case, shorten your hook length to just a few inches.

3 Touch ledgering is the most exciting and efficient way to detect bites. Simply point the rod as directly at the bait as you can, pull the line away from the bottom ring and hold it between your thumb and forefinger. You will find it's easy to hold the rod in one hand and feel for the bites in the other. Strike as soon as you feel a sharp tug or a slow draw on the line. It's almost impossible to put into words the sort of sensation I'm trying to describe, but practice will very soon make you perfect. It sounds almost like magic at first, but it's a method I now use whenever I can.

FISHING WITH BREAD

It's often worth taking a large unsliced loaf to one of the long, featureless straights on your river. At first, this stretch of water may not look very promising. Start, however, pulling small pieces of crust from the loaf and throwing them out into mid river. Watch

carefully as they float off down stream. If there's a chub population about, there is a good chance that the fish will be attracted up in a few minutes after 10 or so crusts have drifted over their heads. You will soon see action – bow waves, big splashes, loud sucks. It's exciting stuff, and all you need to do is put a matchbox-sized piece of crust on a size 4 hook, wet it just a little, and then flick it underarm out into the current. Let it float down naturally until you see it engulfed. Don't strike immediately or you'll pull the bait out of the chub's lips – wait for the line to draw tight.

◄ LEDGERED BREAD
Even a floating bait can be ledgered. With this rig, the buoyant bread crust will hover a few inches above the bed of the river, held in position by the weight of the ledger.

⋏ TAKING IT EASY

If you are going to use a quiver tip for bite indication, then you do need a good, strong rod rest that will hold the rod stable. A comfortable chair is also a good idea for a long-stay session. Make sure that you have all your gear spread around you and that you know where everything is. Quiver tipping works particularly well on slower, deeper runs like this one. The dog is optional!

⋎ RIVER GLORY

I love photographs like this, where the focus is on the beauty of the fish in the loveliness of its natural environment. This European barbel was caught on a bunch of lobworms.

CHUB AT LONG RANGE

This series of pictures shows me solving a problem. I'd seen a group of chub at long range, under a line of alder trees. The dense branches meant that I couldn't get close to the fish and swing a bait through to them. So I was forced a long way upstream – about 60 yards – and had to devise a way of getting a bait down there. A very big float was needed. It had to be big to support a large bait that would be easily visible. I used a long rod of around 13 feet (4m) and line of about 5 pounds (2.2kg) breaking strain. Strong line is vital when you're trying to bring a big fish back against the flow of a river.

It's a good idea to throw in a few samples of the bait first, to bring the chub out from under the tree branches or other snags. So, the plan was set...

⋏ BAITING UP

Take a fresh slice of white bread. Pull out a piece the size of a large coin. Push the hook through the bread and then press the bread gently but firmly around the shank. Leave all the edges nice and loose so pieces break off in the current.

⋎ EASY DOES IT

Long casting isn't called for in this particular instance and all you need to do is swing the bait out into the current underarm. This way you achieve nice control and the pendulum action leaves the bread secure on the hook.

⋏ HOLDING BACK

It's a good idea now and again to stop paying out line behind the float as it trots off down current. This means that the float is held in the water and the bread actually lifts up through the water layers toward the surface.

↗ FISH ON
A hundred yards downstream, the float has dipped under. A good, sweeping strike has to be made so that all the slack line is tightened and the hook is set. The clutch of the reel is quite tight so that line isn't given too easily.

◄ THE BATTLE
Once a fish is hooked, draw it firmly away from the rest of the shoal. Keep drawing it up river, winding in as soon as you can gain any slack.

↗ EASY AS SHE COMES
Remember to guide the fish into the net, then gently lift. Don't hurry. If you splash the net, you'll only alarm the fish into a final lunge.

⌄ MINOR SURGERY
This is where your forceps come in. You'll find that you can take the hook out easily – especially if the hook is barbless. This should cause the fish no discomfort.

⌄ AND BACK SHE GOES
Look at the fish for a few seconds and drink in its beauty. Then hold the fish steady in the water until strength returns. She'll soon tell you when it's time to go.

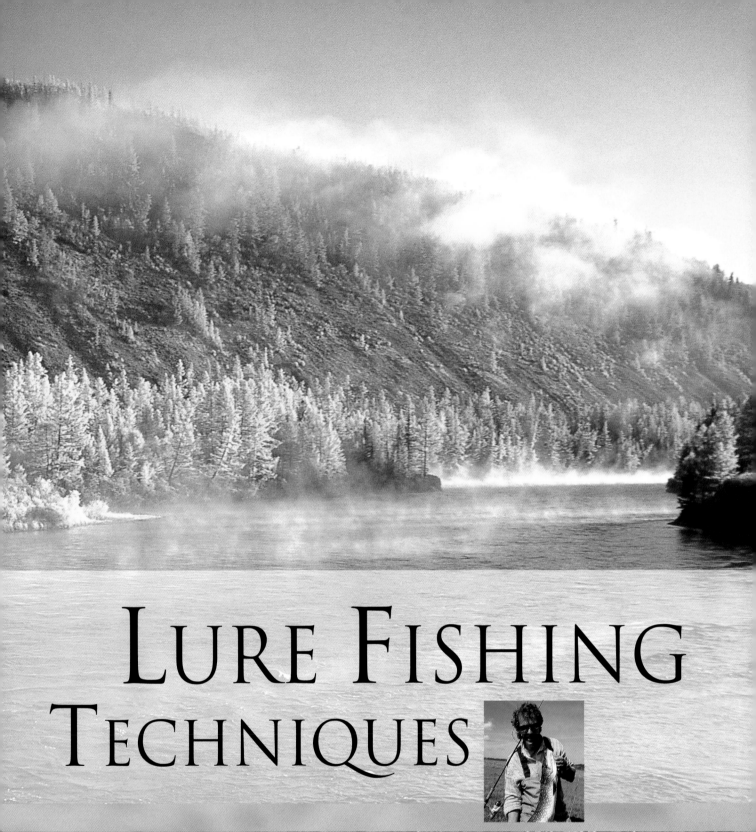

LURE FISHING
TECHNIQUES

Lure Fishing Techniques

Ne of the appealing things about lure fishing is that you have to keep both your body and your mind mobile; if you slip into a mindless, automatic way of fishing, then you're not going to catch much at all.

Always try to travel light. The rod, reel, perhaps a landing net, and a light bag with lures and accessories are really all you need. Don't weigh yourself down with too much equipment, because you'll become less and less enthusiastic about moving, and it's only by searching that you'll locate the fish. If it's winter time, dress warmly, with something to cover your head, and you're ready to fish.

As a general rule, if you're not getting any action, then move on. Search all likely areas and if there's no joy, either fish aren't present or

they're not feeding. A generalization I know, but it's all you can really do. Conversely, if you once hit a single fish – whether landed or not – then do stay put for a while and give the area a real working over. Although we don't think of pike, for example, as proper shoaling fish, you will tend to find that a number of specimens will often hole up together and form a tight group. This doesn't always happen, but any success is worth exploring further.

What features are we looking for? Basically, you've just got to put yourself into the mindset of a

A THE PROUD ANGLER
This very pretty pike was taken on a floating plug drawn under a canopy of overhanging trees. Pike are always looking for cover.

Y PERFECT COVER
Lily pads are particularly attractive to pike. They like the shade they give from the sun, but lily pads also provide a perfect ambush point. Try working a lure as close to the fringe of the pads as you can.

predator. Imagine that you are the creature mounting an ambush on a passing shoal of fish. You will need cover. Perhaps you'll shelter behind a bridge support, or in the deep, dark water on a bend. Obviously you would want to make use of reed and weedbeds, lilies, sunken boats – anything that breaks up your menacing form and renders you as invisible as possible.

Remember this when you are casting your lure. Try to place it as accurately as possible, and as close as you can to the various structures that you have in mind. Work your lure for as long as possible, along a reed bed, for example, or past some sunken pilings.

Don't rush anything... give an uncertain predator time to make its mind up. The more you think about what you are doing, the more you experiment, the more you walk and the more places you try, the greater your chances of success.

⋏ A BIG STRIPY

A really big perch like this has a huge mouth quite capable of taking a prey a third of its own body weight! The message is clear: don't be afraid to use a big lure if it's a really big perch that you're after.

THE SINK AND DRAW METHOD

Essentially lure fishing with a deadbait, this is a great way to catch predators.

1 Using a pair of treble hooks on a wire trace, set up a deadbait so that it is slightly curved. This gives it a pleasing, twisting motion through the water.

2 Work the deadbait very much in the way that I've described for lure fishing. Try to impart as much life to the deadbait as you possibly can, but then stop the retrieve and allow it to sink.

3 Let the deadbait lie motionless on the bottom for a couple of minutes. Then begin to twitch it back for say 3 or 4 yards. Then let it settle again and repeat the process.

4 If that doesn't work, try moving the deadbait more rapidly in mid water.

5 If you see fish striking on the surface, cast out the deadbait and then twitch it back very quickly through the surface layers.

◄ A PINPOINT CAST
When you're lure fishing, don't just cast blindly around a lake, but really think where you want your lure to be. In this instance, I was aiming for the gap between some overhanging trees where I was sure fish would be lurking.

➤ SURFACE ATTRACTION
When the day is bright and the water is calm, a lure working close on the surface is especially attractive. It gives out all sorts of vibrations, and a pike can see the ripples easily overhead.

⋎ THE STRIKE
I actually saw the fish leave the shelter of the overhanging branches and arrow across the water after my lure. Its mouth opened and its gills flared a vivid red. The plug simply vanished.

A SURFACE LURE

A dawn in the summer time. A nice warm clear morning, and just the time to try a floating lure. Choose something that really gurgles as you pull it back. Perhaps it will be a propeller blade, fore or aft, that throws off the commotion. Look for shallow water, preferably near sunken weed beds. The chances are that pike, zander, or other predators have come in during the hours of darkness to search for small shoal fish. Cast far, let the ripples spread, and then work the lure intelligently. Don't just pull it back at a steady 3 or 4 miles an hour – vary the retrieve. Stop the retrieve altogether for 3 or 4 seconds, let the lure just hang motionless in the water, and you will find that a lot of pike take at this moment. Look for any surface activity of small fish being chased – a dead give-away that a big predator is on the prowl. A surface lure cast over an area of commotion is likely to be taken at once – and ferociously. Prepare for fireworks.

➤ A REAL SCRAPPER
When the water is clear and warm, you'll find that pike really go. Ensure that your line is in tip-top condition and all your knots are secure.

⚓ A LAST DITCH EFFORT
I was just bringing this pike toward me when it set off again, its body thrashing the surface. If the reel hadn't been able to give line, a break would have been inevitable.

⚓ NETTED AT LAST
A big, deep landing net is important for fish as big as this. If your net isn't deep enough, you run the risk of the fish leaping out as you wade ashore.

⚓ BE CONFIDENT
The mouth of a pike can look very scary with all those wicked, wolflike teeth but if you take your time, the hooks are easily removed. Place the pike on its back and slip your hand under the gill cover. You'll find that the mouth opens easily, and with a long pair of forceps you can remove the hooks. Once again, always make sure they're barbless.

⚓ A GENTLE RELEASE
Hold the fish in the water until it's strong enough to swim away of its own accord. Now is the perfect time to look at your capture and take in the splendour of its subtle markings.

103

A A PERCH IN THE AUTUMN
This is a very big perch indeed. It fell to a small deadbait fished hard on the bottom when the weather was cold and the water was murky. Conditions like this do not make for very good lure fishing.

➤ JIGGING PARADISE
The scene is one of the huge, clear, cold Baltic lakes where pike proliferate. Jigging with rubber lures is particularly successful here, and a boatload of anglers is working a known hot spot. Use different types and colours of jig until the going pattern for the day is found.

△ JIG SUCCESS
This lovely pike came just as the jig hit bottom and was twitched up to begin the retrieve. You can catch pike at any stage when jigging – when the jig is moving down towards the bottom or up toward the surface.

▼ RED LETTER DAYS
This is truly a beautiful pike, but look how carefully it is being cradled for the photograph. Don't be afraid of these big predators, even though their mouths do look pretty scary.

FISHING WITH RUBBER LURES

Perhaps there's no more exciting way of fishing for perch than by using rubber lures close to obvious structures in the water.

Choose your fishing position carefully – you want to be close to the landing stage, the boathouse, that sunken boat, those flooded pilings… anything that is going to attract a shoal of perch.

You don't want to have to cast a long way but simply flick the rubber lure out, let it sink down to the bottom, and then twitch it up and down, backwards and forwards until you get some sort of indication. Do your twitching – or jigging as it's commonly called – intelligently. Just like working any lure, it doesn't pay to be mechanical. Try to inject as much life into your rubber as you possibly can!

Try different rubber shapes, colours, and sizes. If a worm doesn't work, try a lizard or even a little squid. Perch are great investigators, and you'll often find that they'll come close and study a lure for several minutes before making a decision. Often, changing the lure just a fraction in terms of shape, size or colour will trigger an immediate response.

Sometimes you will find that the rubbers are just nipped a little or tugged. In these circumstances, it pays perhaps to trim a little bit off the tail. Do this in tiny fractions so the action isn't overly compromised. Or, you might try nicking a small worm on the hook to give that added sense of realism, and perhaps an increased odour.

See what I mean about lure fishing being for the intelligent, thinking angler? It's all about deception, and fish are very frequently less easily deceived than you would initially believe.

the spoon working its way along the bottom, occasionally bouncing into a dead lily pad, for example, or just spurting over a patch of sand. Takes tend to be very solid, and at first you might think that you've hooked into a snag. This will happen, of course, but just as frequently that snag will fight back!

DEADBAITS

Lure fishing is a tremendously exciting way of catching predators, but it does depend to quite a great degree on relatively clear water. If your river or lake is clouded, then lure fishing has to be queried in terms of effectiveness. This is the moment that you've really got to try something else, and this will probably be deadbaiting.

Ensure that your deadbaits are as fresh as possible. Pike are not scavengers, and they do like a succulent meal. Always go for dead sea fish rather than dead freshwater fish. Taking freshwater fish can seriously damage stocks in some freshwater fisheries.

It pays to have a variety of baits with you – herring, mackerel, sardines and sprats are favourites, but any other sea fish that you might find on the fishmonger's slab are all worth a bash – especially on pressured fisheries where pike have seen most things before.

Once again, make sure that your trebles have squashed barbs and, above all, strike very quickly once a run develops. If you do miss a pike on the strike, then in all probability it's a very small fish that hasn't been able to mouth the bait properly. If it's a decent pike, then it will almost always be hooked as soon as a run develops. Deadbaiting can occasionally seem slow work but there are ways of livening it up (see opposite).

⚓ LOOKING FOR DINNER
This marauding pike has picked up the scent of the deadbait lying close to it. In quite murky water like this, it might take a few minutes for the pike to home in on its prey. Pike do have good eyesight, but if the water is cloudy, then scent becomes vital for survival.

⌄ A FLOAT-FISHED DEADBAIT
When the water is murky, deadbaiting really comes into its own, and half a dead mackerel like this gives off a lot of oily odours into the water. Fish a mackerel or any sea fish hard on the bottom with a float set so that it rides proud on the surface. Half deadbaits are particularly good because they let out more of the juices. Always remember to use a wire trace when you're fishing for predators with teeth.

LURE FISHING IN WINTER
Now it's winter, and there's even thin ice on the margins of the lake, the result of several days of severe cold. Predators, pike especially, are lethargic, not inclined to chase food, but possibly willing to snaffle something that comes close and looks vulnerable. This is the time for a deep diving plug, or even a big, heavy spoon. Cast it out, and then crank the plug down until you can feel it hitting bottom. This is excellent; imagine it, down in the depths, churning its way through the bottom silt. Even if the pike can't actually see the lure, it will feel the vibrations through the water and perhaps pick up on the mushrooming clouds of silt. Work the lure as slowly as you can because the big predator won't be in a hurry now that the temperatures have dipped.

You can work a big, silver, flashing spoon in exactly the same sort of fashion. Cast it out and let it sink right down to the bottom. Once no more line is being paid out, then you can afford to retrieve, slowly but in quick bursts, trying to imagine

106

DRIFTING DEADBAITS

Perhaps the most exciting way to fish deadbaits is under a drifter float, set up as the photo (right) shows.

Wind can be a restriction. Ideally, you need a force three or above.

The great advantage of the drifter float is that you check out all the water from close into the bank, right out to a hundred yards plus.

The weighting of the rig has to be precise. Too little weight, and the drifter float will flop over on its side. Too great a weight, and the drifter float will sink so that too little of the vane is standing proud to catch the wind.

Make sure that the line from the float to the rod tip is well greased to keep it afloat. You can buy an automatic greasing device for this.

Stop the float fairly frequently on its trip out across the water. Simply shut the bale arm to prevent extra line being given out. This will have the effect of moving the float

several yards either left or right, and in this way even more water is being covered.

Once the float gets to a good distance – over 60 or 70 yards (55–64m) for example – your binoculars will probably be neeeded. Watch the float very carefully indeed for any sign of a taking fish. Do not delay on striking because the fish could swallow the bait and then unhooking becomes a nightmare.

When striking, wind down until the line is tight to the taking fish. Then lift the rod and walk backwards up the bank, striking as you go. This action sets the hook even at very long range. Always make sure that your reel is filled to the very lip if you are drift floating. Sometimes you will be fishing well in excess of 150 yards (135m) away, and if a fish then runs another 20 yards (18m) away from you, you could be in trouble unless you have plenty of line to spare.

➤ THE DRIFTER RIG

If you want to search out big areas of water, then it's a good idea to use a drifter float if there's anything like a breeze. See the big vane on the float: this catches the wind and pushes the float and bait across the water. Set the float so the bait is riding about mid-way between surface and bed. Use a lead big enough to cock the float nicely so that just the vane and the shoulder of the float are showing above the surface.

⌄ SCOTTISH GLORY

This lovely pike was taken from a Scottish loch in the springtime. It is lean after spawning, and was very hungry when it came across a trout deadbait.

FLY CASTING
TECHNIQUES

FLY CASTING TECHNIQUES

B EGINNERS OFTEN TEND TO LOOK ON FLY CASTING AS SOME SORT OF SECRET, HIDDEN ART, BUT IT'S NOT LIKE THAT AT ALL. THE BASIC CAST IS EASY TO LEARN IN JUST AN HOUR OR TWO.

To be positive, fly casting is a very satisfying physical experience in itself, and you don't always need to catch a fish during the day to enjoy the sport you've had.

There are literally scores of different types of cast, but most are variations on a theme. Providing that you can master the simple overhead cast, one that will be used in 90 percent of situations, then you are well on the way. You'll soon discover that when you find yourself in tricky corners, under trees for example, then you will instinctively begin to side cast, using the know-how that you've already put together.

But what are the steps to good casting? Well, the first consideration is to make sure that the rod and line are matched and are strong enough for the job in hand. Lines are important: one that is covered in sand, shingle, or mud will not glide through the rings nearly as well as one that is kept clean and greased. Check rod rings frequently to make sure there are no grooves to slow down the line speed through them.

The general, basic overhead cast depends on a number of things. Firstly, you've got to consider the speed of the line that is obtained by moving the rod forwards and

> DISTANCE WITH ACCURACY
It's probable that the fish are quite a distance in front of this angler. Casting has to be more forceful than it is on a small river, but that doesn't mean to say that accuracy and delicacy are not important.

⩘ PINPOINT STUFF
This shot was taken on New Zealand's south island and it shows an angler stalking big rainbow trout in a tiny stream that's crystal clear. Any false move would result in a startled, bolting fish. Fishing up stream is also recommended simply because it is less easy for a trout to see an angler coming from behind him.

⩗ IN THE UNDERGROWTH
It's surprising how accurately you can fish a small, overgrown river if you take your time and look carefully around you at where trees are hanging and bankside vegetation growing. Move slowly and cast careful, short lines. Don't go for distance but concentrate on accuracy. This type of fishing is best begun on calm days.

SAFETY CONSIDERATIONS

1 You will already have picked up throughout this book that I'm a firm believer in anglers wearing polarizing glasses at all times, because you can see so much more through the surface of the water. When fly casting, this is especially important, as you want to target your fish as accurately as possible. They also help you to see the river bed when wading, and may prevent you stepping into a deep hole!

2 The eye protection that glasses offer is vital, too. Remember that you have a hooked artificial fly traveling round and round your head and body all day long, frequently at great speeds. There is that ever-distinct possibility – however remote – that a gust of wind could blow it directly at your face. I've seen people with hooks in their noses and ears, and I've had one in my scalp. That's bad

enough, but the thought of a hook in the eye… wear those glasses.

3 To avoid hooking yourself, always check wind speed and direction. Be very wary of a wind that is blowing the fly line actually toward you. If you're right-handed, this obviously means a wind coming from the right. Try to avoid such a situation, especially when you're a beginner.

4 Once again, as in nearly all forms of fishing, use a barbless hook or flatten the barb when you're fly fishing. Should anything go wrong, a barbless hook slips out with relatively little pain or fuss.

5 Always check above and behind you for any power lines. Remember how easily electricity is conducted through carbon.

6 When you are fly fishing, always be aware of anybody moving behind you

along the bank. Never risk that quick cast before they arrive, just in case you get your timing wrong.

7 Whenever you move position, it's a good idea to look behind you to see if there are any problematic trees or bushes… or livestock! I've actually seen a young bullock hooked in the ear and run off all the line and backing!

8 If you're wading on a river or stillwater, it's frequently tempting to go out just that little bit further and deeper to reach rising fish. Do this very, very carefully, and always make sure that you're well within your depth. If you are wading, it's a good idea to have a wading stick with you to act as a third leg for balance, and also to be able to test depths in front. Be extra careful if there is a rapid current.

backwards – false casting – and gives real power and velocity. This is partly obtained by the leverage of the rod and the power of your wrist, which together produce a type of catapult effect. The speed that the line travels can be increased by pulling on the line above the reel and below the bottom ring. The downward pull simply increases the line speed and therefore adds a bit of distance. Don't worry about this at the start, but consider it once you're getting the hang of things.

One of the most frequent reasons for failure is not maintaining the speed of the fly line, and one of the major faults is allowing the line to fall slack on its backwards movement. The cast will certainly fall if it is not taut and in control on the back cast.

This is really important, and for this reason it's beneficial if the beginner looks at his back cast as he is making it. This might seem ungainly and not particularly professional, but at least you're assuring yourself that the line is stretching out nicely and that you're ready for the forwards cast, which will deliver the fly correctly.

Casting instructors for decades have put the fly rod against a clock face: the idea is that your back cast stops at one o'clock on the face and your forward cast stops when the rod is at 11 o'clock. This concept has a lot going for it. If the rod moves in the arc between 10 o'clock and two o'clock, you will find that your line frequently begins to sag and you lose control. If your back cast goes down to three o'clock, for example, there's

hardly any chance of getting the line back into the air once more. Part of the reason for this is the amount of air pressure that builds up on the line and the consequent slowing down of the line's speed… but that's probably more technical information than we need so let's simply stick to the rules. The basic principle, therefore, is to keep the rod moving between the 11 o'clock and the one o'clock positions – false casting again – so that you can get more line to place the fly further away from the bankside.

Always remember to keep the line tight in your left hand as you are casting. If you let the line go slack for any reason, then velocity and power are obviously lost and the whole cast will lose its momentum.

FLY CASTING

1 GETTING STARTED
Hold the fly in your left hand while you pull some line off the reel. Then flick the line and the fly into the water.

2 PULLING LINE OFF THE REEL
The next step is to pull a yard (1m) or so of line off the reel. Shake the rod so that this line runs through the rings.

3 REPEAT THE PROCESS
Pull off more line and again waggle the rod so that it follows down through into the water. You'll now have enough line out to start a cast.

7 GETTING READY TO GO LONG
The first short cast is completed and the extra fly line can be seen clearly now hanging beneath the reel.

8 GOING FOR A LONG CAST
The line is picked up off the water as the rod goes backwards. Let the extra line go through your fingers.

9 KEEP YOUR EYE ON THAT FLY
You've now got about 10 yards (9m) of line behind you. For the first cast or so look behind to make sure that the line straightens properly.

PROBLEM BUSTING

Despite everything, your casting is not really progressing as you'd like. Let's have a look at some possible solutions.

1 Are you sure your rod and line are matched? It's no good using a heavy rod with a light line, or vice versa.

2 Is your back cast working properly? Are you letting it open out nicely behind you so that it's pretty well straight and level before you begin your forward cast? If you're letting that back cast droop and fall toward the ground, then you're in trouble.

3 Is the line traveling with enough speed? Beginners often appear to be frightened of the whole process and perhaps don't attack the job with enough vim and vigour! Of course you can overdo this, but it's better to err on the positive side than the negative.

4 It could be that your fly is simply too heavy to cast successfully. Very big lures do demand special casting techniques. It's far better to start off with a small nymph tied on a size 14 or 16 hook, perhaps.

5 Are you trying to push your fly into too strong a wind? If there is much wind, it's easier to have the wind behind you. If it's blowing straight into your face, then even an expert will have problems. It is best to go out the first few times in conditions that are as calm as possible.

6 Is your leader – the length of nylon line that attaches your fly to the main fly line – too long? In very specialized conditions, it's a good idea to have a long leader, but when you're beginning, don't tie one up that's longer than your rod. If, for example, you're using a 9 foot (2.7m) rod, then an 8 or 9 foot (2.4–2.7m) leader is about right.

7 Are you being too ambitious, making too many false casts and trying to get just a few too many yards of line? At first, style and technique are more important than distance. Providing your casting is tight and neat, it doesn't really matter if you are getting out 7 yards of line or 17 yards. It's better to concentrate on good short casting to start with rather than going for wild, long casts that are probably landing noisily and scaring fish away. You will find that your distance builds up gradually the more times you go out.

8 It could be that your fly line is sticky for some reason. Strip it off the reel and give it a good wash in warm, slightly soapy water. You'll be surprised at how much dirt and grit comes off. Once clean, you will find that your line slides much more easily through the rings.

4 FALSE CASTING
False casting is all about moving your rod backwards and forwards as you get more and more fly line out into the air.

5 START SHORT
After one or two false casts, let the fly land seven or eight yards (6.5–7.5m) in front of you. There could be a fish close into the bank.

6 MORE LINE OUT
At the end of this first short cast, pull more line off your reel – about another two yards (1.8m) or so.

10 OUT IT GOES
On your forwards cast, the whole 10 or 11 yards (9–10m) of line shoots out and lands gently in the river before you.

11 A STEADY RETRIEVE
As the fly swings round in the current, keep the line tight by pulling in any slack with your left hand.

12 STARTING OVER
You've now got quite a bit of line in your left hand and you're raising the rod to cast again. Keep everything smooth and controlled.

FLY FISHING
TECHNIQUES

FLY FISHING TECHNIQUES

S O, YOU'VE GOT THE RIGHT GEAR AND YOU CAN CAST A FLY WITH REASONABLE ACCURACY TO A FISHABLE DISTANCE. WHAT NEXT? WELL, THE GOLDEN RULE BEHIND FLY FISHING IS TO 'MATCH THE HATCH'. WHAT THE FLY ANGLER MEANS BY THIS IS IMITATING THE NATURAL INSECT AS NEARLY AS POSSIBLE WITH THE ARTIFICIAL.

The master plan is to fool the trout into thinking that fur and feather are the real, living creatures.

To do this expertly, it means being able to identify pretty well exactly what the majority of trout are feeding on, at any particular moment. You then, hopefully, have the right artificial in your fly box to join the swarm of naturals.

This is a skill that you build through experience, so don't worry if, at first, this all seems a little bit inaccessible. Time and perseverance will heal all that, and there will be

⋎ A THRILLING MOMENT
The sight every angler wants to see – a lovely brown trout is nosing its way up through flowing weed ready to engulf a mayfly pattern.

⋎ CHOICE OF FLY
Choice of fly really can be important, especially on large stillwaters when it's very clear, very hot and there's very little wind. It really pays to ask advice from somebody who knows, and here I am talking to a fishery manager. Big fly or small fly? Light or dark? You need to know.

many times in the fly fishing season when you will get it right, and 'matching the hatch' won't seem too difficult at all. If you manage to do the thing properly once or twice, your confidence will build up, as will your desire to know more.

So, let's look at a few scenarios, tailor-made for the newcomer.

For our first scenario, it's late May or early June on a clear, pristine trout river. Sit quietly and just watch the river and the reed beds around. The chances are that after a while you will begin to see large iridescent flies on the surface of the water that slowly spiral off into the air above. These

flies will be an inch or more in height, and will be coloured a glowing white, yellow or green. Sometimes, you'll just see them singly or in very small groups, but there will be periods throughout the day when the river absolutely swarms with these glorious insects. When this happens, the trout will be going mad. What you are witnessing is one of the golden periods in any trout fisherman's calendar… the mayfly hatch.

The mayfly is just so big and juicy that even wary, old trout often throw caution to the wind, and for this reason the two weeks of the mayfly season were often referred to as the 'Duffer's Fortnight'. And it's true. Rarely are trout so easily caught at any other time of the season. It's a truly a wonderful time to be out on the riverbank.

For the general run of trout, you needn't be too picky about which mayfly you select from your box, though obviously if you get the size and colour right, it's going to be a big advantage for you.

Cast as gently as you can, about a yard (1m) or so upstream of any steadily feeding trout that you have observed, and try and let the fly drift down towards it without the current dragging it off course. It pays, obviously, to get well downstream of the rising trout so that the effect of the current is minimized.

When you do get a rise, never be in too great a hurry to strike: this is a big insect and even a pound and a half trout will take a little time to completely envelop it in its mouth. Try counting to three before tightening. If that doesn't work, try two or four, and so on. To catch your first trout on a dry fly is a momentous achievement and there's no finer way of doing it than during the peak of the mayfly season.

◀ AN IMITATION MAYFLY
Remember that you are trying to do two things: first, you are trying to present an artificial fly that looks a little like the real thing. Secondly, you are trying to make it behave as naturally as possible.

▼ OBSERVATION
You need to watch the water both to see where the fish are lying and, hopefully, to get some idea of what they're feeding on. Are they down deep taking nymphs? If they are, you'll often see the whites of their mouths as the lips open and shut. Or are they on the surface sipping down hatching insects?

FLY FISHING TIPS

1 Always buy (or make) two flies of each type, size and colour: it's so irritating to have found the winning fly on a particular day only to lose it in an overhanging tree.

2 If you can't match the natural flies and nymphs perfectly, don't worry too much – it's how the fly behaves in the water that matters just as much as how it looks.

3 Always try to think how the natural fly does behave, and attempt to make your artificial work in the same sort of way. So don't twitch methodically, but vary how you retrieve your fly. Put a bit of imagination into it, and concentrate all the time. Results will rocket.

4 It's probably true to say that 90 percent of takes are never even guessed at by the angler. A trout can swim up, suck in a fly, and then reject it without the angler having a clue what's happened. For this reason, keep everything tight to the fly and watch both your line and your leader with hawk-like concentration. Strike if you think anything is amiss, and you can often be rewarded.

5 Very often anglers use bite indicators – little pieces of putty or polystyrene – on the line to help with bite indication. These act like floats in bait fishing. They are especially useful when fishing for grayling in winter on rivers. Always consider having a packet with you for very difficult situations.

6 One of the most useful tricks in nymph fishing is the induced take. The idea here is that you can see a trout looking at your nymph beneath the surface. It can't make its mind up, so you do it for it. You do this by twitching the nymph quite vigorously at precisely the moment the trout comes to investigate. The nymph rises 6 inches (15cm) or so in the water and this triggers an instant reaction in the trout. Woof! You are suddenly playing your fish.

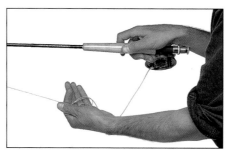

⋏ A CAREFUL RETRIEVE
At times, when you want to inch your imitation back through the water, it's vital not to have a lot of loose line dangling around. This is where folding it back into your palm can be useful.

BUZZERS

Next, picture a lake in the evening, probably after a warm day. A slight scum has built up during the daylight hours, and now there's a thick surface film to the water. Watch the water in front of you – the chances are that you will see bulges in this glutinous covering. You might also hear a distinctive sucking sound. These are definite signs of trout, and you may see the back of the fish break surface or, at least, the tip of the dorsal or tail fin. These trout are taking buzzers, the common term for hatching midges. The bloodworm rise from the bottom of the lake,

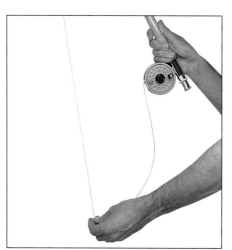

⋏ THE INDUCED TAKE
A trout is following your nymph. Pause, lift the rod and pull the fly line down with your left hand. The nymph will rise in the water as though it's about to escape. The trout just can't resist!

ascend to the surface, where they struggle out of their pupal cases. As they do so, they are left defenceless for a few minutes, and the trout feast on them. At this time, the trout are very catchable.

Reach for the row of buzzers in the fly box. Perhaps start with a red one, with a white, hairy head tied on a size 16. Don't fish too heavy a hook length: around 3 to 4 pounds (1.3–1.8kg) breaking strain at the point is about right, depending on the size of the trout in the lake. It pays also to grease your leader up to about 3 inches (7cm) away from the fly itself. This will make the nylon float, and you need to watch this for a sign of a take. Cast the buzzer out as close to the activity as you can. If you take your time, it's often possible to watch the course of a single, feeding fish. If you manage to do this, try to place your fly about 4 or 5 feet (1.2–1.5m) in front of where the trout is heading. Let everything settle, and watch that greased line like a hawk, though this can be difficult in low light conditions. Keep everything as tight as you can, trying to keep direct contact with that buzzer. If you see a fish approaching the general area, try twitching the buzzer back toward you, 1 or 2 inches (3–5cm) at a time until you've worked the fly back perhaps 4 or 5 feet (1.2–1.5m) towards the bank.

Takes can be very gentle indeed. You might just see the nylon of your leader edge forward minutely. Or, if the trout takes the buzzer during your twitch period you'll often feel it take with a distinct tug. Lift your rod tip and strike immediately.

⋗ A REAL TEST
This beautiful rainbow trout, caught on the River Test in England, was landed on a mayfly pattern in early June. The day was cloudy and the mayfly kept on hatching steadily. Perfect.

◣ TOP OF THE MORNING
It's a lovely day and the lake is mine. Where do I begin? I look for a bay or rippled water. That island is nice but it's rather too long a cast! I think I'll head towards the rushes.

ENTICING TROUT WITH A LURE
Late summer now, perhaps in the afternoon, and you notice trout swimming quickly in the surface film, often with very small fish sheering out in front of them. These trout are almost certainly taking fry and small fish from close to the surface. Time now to try a lure. Choose one from your box that resembles any small, flashing fish. Tie it onto a heavier than usual leader since trout will take flies like this with hammer force. Then, cast your fly out as far as you can into the area of general activity. Pause for a few seconds while the fly sinks, then begin to retrieve it back towards you, your left hand pulling at the fly line in 2–6 inch (5–15cm) short, sharp bursts. Very often, you'll see the wake of a trout following the fly

◢ FAST RETRIEVE
I'm kicking off with quite a large fly that I hope will look like a small fish. This requires quite a fast retrieve and I'm pulling 6 inches (15cm) of line or so through my fingers at a time.

◥ A BELTING TAKE
When you are retrieving a fly quickly, the trout have to accelerate to take it. The result is a take that really bends the rod. The hook is often set before you need to think of striking.

⋏ COMING TO HAND
The battle is just about done after a fast and furious five minutes. I'm bending down so the fish doesn't see me and take fright, and also because then I can just guide it to my hands.

⋏ A SWIFT RELEASE
The fish is now lying in the shallow water at my feet and it's a simple matter to reach for the forceps and slide the barbless hook shank out of the fish's jaw.

➤ ONE FOR THE CAMERA
As this fish is so beautiful, I'm lifting it out of the water with wet hands for a quick picture. Treat the fish gently, and you'll find they swim off strongly, the wiser for their experience.

itself. Exciting stuff, and it pays to actually speed the rate of retrieve up rather than letting it fall off.

Make half a dozen casts with your first choice lure, and then change it if there's no activity. Six more casts, then change again until you find the fly that the fish are willing to take on the day. And watch out for that take… as I've said, trout hit lures with a force that sends a shiver down your spine.

FLY FISHING WITH A NYMPH

Let's say now that you're on a river or a clear stillwater in the middle of the day and nothing is moving on the surface. Still, you've got your Polaroids, you're willing to spend time watching, and you've got some idea about moving as cautiously as you can along the bankside. Look down deep, and you'll probably see trout moving around. If they're lying still, then possibly they're not feeding, but any sign of movement indicates that these are busy fish. Look even more carefully, and from time to time you'll see the whites of the inside of their mouths. You see this flash because they have opened their mouths to swallow something – more often than not some passing nymph. And it's a nymph, therefore, that you'll be using to tempt these deep, feeding fish.

⋏ OUT ON THE RIVER
Always make use of every available scrap of bankside cover. Fish a short, tight line and move carefully and slowly up-river, watching for your fish. Those are the keys to success.

But which nymph? In all probability, the trout aren't feeding on anything in particular but simply looking for small creatures that fit a general picture. Try kicking off with one of the most tried and tested of all nymphs – the Pheasant Tail. This brown, weighted imitation is probably best tied on a size 14 or 16 hook. If you're on a river, cast this about a yard (1m) or so upstream of the trout that you've watched feeding.

⋏ A LITTLE BEAUTY
This is a wild brown trout caught from a lowland English stream, something comparatively rare nowadays. It may be small, but it's very precious and very beautiful.

➢ RIVER FROM HEAVEN
This is the magnificent River Itchin down in Hampshire, England. Its crystal waters and abundant weed growth help breed the most wonderful stocks of wild brown trout.

You've got to consider how deep the trout is lying though – if it's lying very deep, the nymph will take longer to sink. If it's near the surface, then obviously not as much time will be needed. This sort of current/depth calculation does take time to perfect, but you'll manage it sooner than you think. Watch your leader or even the fly line once again very carefully. If it stops, strike. If it shoots forward, strike. It's like magic when you lift into that first nymph-caught trout.

⅄ HIGHLAND MAGIC

It's late afternoon in the highlands. There's a good wind blowing insects off the moorland. This is the time to try a floating line blowing along with a large imitation bouncing on the surface – something like a Daddy Long Legs pattern is ideal. Keep moving after every two or three casts until you find a different fish.

TAKING FLY FISHING FURTHER

We've only really had time to talk about fairly standard fly fishing situations, but there's a whole world waiting out there for the fly rodder.

1 You could try dapping live mayfly as well as imitations on the beautiful limestone loughs of western Ireland – an amazing experience.

2 You'll probably want to try fly fishing for salmon at some stage. An exciting moment, whether it be on the big rivers of Canada, the intimate rivers of Devon, or the majestic rivers of Norway.

3 The chalk stream experience is one not to be missed. It is possible to buy day tickets on the really famous rivers such as the Test in England. If you get the opportunity, go for it. These rivers are a trout fisher's paradise.

4 How about steelhead in British Columbia? These are sea going rainbow trout that can weigh well in excess of 30 pounds (13.5kg). They fight like demons… and all this in the beautiful land of the elk and the bear. Spectacular.

5 Night is falling on a twinkling, Swedish river. The sea trout will soon be on the move, encouraged by the onset of darkness. You wade in the inky silence, feeling your way, casting under the moonlight. Then… bang… your heart almost stops with excitement.

6 You are high on the Scottish hills, tramping through the heather, watched only by the red stags. Your target is a small lochen or a tiny burn, home to miniature, wild brown trout. Small they may be, but their shape and colouring is so perfect a hike of 20 miles is worth every footfall.

7 Or perhaps it's bonefish you're seeking… one of the most hard-fighting fish in the world, even though they rarely weigh more than 7 or 8 pounds (3.2–3.6kg). You will find these stunningly beautiful fish in the shallow, coastal strips around islands such as the Bahamas, Cuba, or even the Seychelles. What could be more stunning… wonderful landscape, the sun on your back and some of the most gripping fishing ever devised?

BASS
FISHING

BASS FISHING

I F THE WORLD OF FRESHWATER HOLDS A MORE DEMANDING AND EXCITING FISH THAN THE BASS, I'VE YET TO MEET IT. WE'RE TALKING ABOUT A REAL TURN-ON SPECIES THAT'S BEEN THROWING DOWN THE CHALLENGE TO AMERICAN ANGLERS FOR GENERATIONS.

To begin bass fishing, your basic gear doesn't have to be that hi-tec. A light rod and matching reel – probably a small multiplier – and you're well on your way. The big issue is finding the fish, and then deciding the right technique to use given the weather, the water conditions, and the fishing situation. Bait? Fly? Lure? Bass fishing is the sport of the 10,000 approaches…

The weather is warm in the high summer and the bass are under the pads. You might just see them there, their tails appearing every now and again, or the lilies themselves lifting up and shaking as the fish shelter from the brightest of the light. The bass probably aren't too hungry at this time, but their eye is always open to a quick and easily won meal. You could consider this a time to go rubber! Try a plastic worm, lizard, snake, or frog. Cast it into any opening and twitch in tiny abrupt spurts. Let it rest. Lift the rod tip so that the creature shakes and shudders and sends out tell-tale ripples. No luck? If the water's very clear go tiny – a little squid, of just an inch or two, perhaps. Or, if there's a lunker of a largemouth down there, go the whole hog with a snake the length of your rod butt. Rest the bass in between attempts – over fishing just spooks them and sends them down or out of the area altogether. A softly-softly approach is almost guaranteed to be the right one.

BASS FISHER'S GLOSSARY

BLACK BASS – the family name for both largemouth and smallmouth bass. Also included are other members such as spotted and redeye bass.

BOBBER – a plastic float designed to register bites and suspend baits at any level in the water.

BRONZE BACK – a regional name for smallmouth bass.

COVER – a feature that provides shade and offers a food supply. Tree roots, bulrushes, fallen trees, and big rocks are all examples of cover.

CRANK BAITS – shallow and deep running plugs. You can cast them a long distance, and you work them back quickly. Their big lips ward off obstructions. Crank baits are ideal for fishing in snaggy areas such as rocks.

FLIPPIN – the word given to an accurate underhand cast. You control the line in your left hand for pinpoint accuracy. Excellent when fishing close to structure and cover.

FLOAT TUBE – sometimes called a belly boat. You sit in something resembling a huge tractor tyre and paddle yourself

around a stillwater. This allows you to get in close to feeding bass.

POPPER – a fly with a cupped or flattened face. This structure allows the fly to skip along the surface imitating a frog or a mouse. Its rubber legs make it very lifelike.

SPINNER BAIT – a very flashy type of spinner with big skirts and extra blades for vibration and colour.

STRUCTURE – the topography of a lake or stream bed. Channels, rocks, drop-offs, and so on are all very attractive to bass.

➤ GIVE THEM PLASTIC

A typical selection of small plugs and spinners that will all raise bass on their day. The important thing is to experiment. You will only need a wire trace if there are pike, muskies, or walleye in the water. And don't forget those forceps. You want to be able to slip the hook out and get that bass back with the least fuss.

➤ GIVE THEM RUBBER

If they won't go for plastic, try a rubber fish, frog, squid, or whatever. Using little jigs like this really does work. Hook one up, drop it over the side, and see how lifelike it looks.

➤ AND THEN THERE'S THE FLY!

You can catch bass on all manner of flies – they needn't necessarily be big streamers like these. Sometimes little imitative flies do just as well. Still, when things get really tough, these are a fly pattern no bass can ignore!

JIGGING

You've located bass closely tucked in amongst the branches and roots of a big, dead tree. Here, the bass can shelter from big predators, as well as mount ambushes of their own on passing prey fish. But they are hugging the wood so close that fishing a running plug isn't a real option at all. Instead, you can try jigging a small spoon. Get your boat as close to the tree as possible and then let your jig spoon down through the layers, twitching it up and down a foot or so at different levels. It pays to hit bottom, knowing the spoon kicks up just a handful of dust and dirt down there – enough in itself to attract an inquisitive bass to investigate. Search the entire depth carefully. Don't be in too much of a hurry to leave, and sometimes let your spoon just hang idle with no movement at all.

No luck? Then perhaps it's worth trying a different sized jig or one with a differently coloured tail. Black and yellow can score, but so can red. Just keep trying. You can also tip your jigs with all manner of things to give them that little bit more

⋏ GETTING AFLOAT
If you can get a boat out onto the water, then you really are a couple of steps ahead. This cast is made toward a big branch that is lying in the water almost coming to the surface. A perfect place for a bass or two to be lurking.

⋏ UNDERNEATH THE ARCHES
I've moved in closer now and I'm working a jig right underneath the overhanging trees, where bass could easily be lurking in the shadow, away from the bright sunlight. There's always the chance, too, of a big fly or a bee perhaps falling from the leaves. A welcome addition to their menu.

attraction. Try the tail of a plastic worm perhaps, or even a piece of bacon rind. The important thing is to keep on experimenting until you hit on the right combination.

FLY FISHING FOR BASS

It's really nice summer weather and the hot summer days mean that the bass are much more likely to feed enthusiastically at dawn. It's calm. There's a bit of mist over the shallow water, and the bass are out in force, feeding on small fry and insects of all sorts. Now's the time to try your hand at fly fishing. Above all, you'll need a really careful approach because the bass are in just a few inches, or at most a foot or two, of water. They can sense your presence a mile off, so move like a heron. It's best to take your time getting up close to the fish rather than risking a long, potentially splashy cast that again will send them hurrying from the area. A floating line is probably what you'll

need, but what sort of fly? A fly that imitates any small fish is the sort of thing that you'll be looking for – perhaps a minnow pattern. Or a big nymph pattern, something that roughly imitates all the bugs and insects that are scurrying around the margins. Whichever you choose, work your fly intelligently. Don't just retrieve in a methodical sort of fashion, but go out of your way to put real-life energy into the fly, to fool the bass into believing that your creation of fur or feather is a real, live insect or fish. If you see any surface activity, you might even try a dry fly. Choose something big and bushy, let it settle, and then just twitch it now and again so the bass thinks that it's homing onto a stranded moth or beetle.

➢ THE ULTIMATE PRIZE
It's great to catch bass on any method, but if you can get them on the fly, you'll experience the ultimate. Big flies, small flies, floating flies – bass will have them all if they look realistic, and you don't scare them off in the first place.

⋏ BASS COUNTRY
Whenever you're looking for bass, look for cover. This is a perfect piece of bass pond. Look at the reeds, the weeds, the overhanging trees... just imagine all the small fish that are hiding out there, pulling bass in from more open parts of the lake.

USING A SUFACE PLUG FOR BASS

It's in situations like this that you could also try using a surface plug, a real killer on calm summer mornings and evenings when the bass are here in the shallows. Try a propeller plug – a highly visible body with a blade at one or both ends. These really churn up the water and pull the fish in. No luck again? Try a popper or a chugger, both of which have concave faces that make gurgling sounds when you bring them back towards you. One of my favourites is a top-water crawler, which has a metal lip to make the lure really wiggle and look like a tiny fish in distress. The important thing is to think the situation out and try and try again until you hit on just the right

formula. Always take your time though, and don't rush. Rest the water between each and every approach. Rush things and you become panicky, and your casting becomes wayward and splashy. It's vital to just take your time, cool down, and think your way through any problems that you encounter.

A great many bass professionals swear by any number of plug patterns, and when they open up their boxes, you'll be amazed by the Pandora collection that they've amassed. However, the important thing is where to work the plug in the first place. You can have as many plugs in your box as you like, but unless you're close to the fish, you'll get precious few takes. The thing to

⋏ KICKING UP A STORM

There are times when bass are really looking for creatures passing over their heads. This is where a small plug with propellers comes in. These little critters really kick up a fuss as they come back across the water, looking a like a panicking mouse trying to get back to the bank.

⋎ CASTING OUT

Here I'm on a fairly open water, and I've been float fishing with a 12 foot rod, but the bass are feeding and I've decided to change to the splashy plug, even if the rod isn't ideal.

remember in bass fishing is the word 'structure'. Structure is really only a general word for something in the water that's like a landmark, a feature that attracts the fish for one reason or another. We've already talked about a dead tree and lily pads, for example, but every water has scores of examples of bass-holding structures. For instance, always look for bass under overhanging cliffs where they like to shelter on the edge of underwater caves. Bridges are brilliant partly because the current of the river is deflected here, and there's always a lot of rubble around that makes for many a good hiding place. Any overhead cover is good – try thick vegetation such as bushes or floating weed. Remember that if any kind of feature, such as an old, dead tree, topples into the margins of a great, clear, featureless lake, you'll find half the bass population in that area within the week.

It's also worth thinking about water clarity. Any areas of murky water are bound to attract bass and make it just that little bit more easy to approach them. Perhaps there's an inflowing stream from farmland that's clouding the water a bit. Investigate it. Bass will be around. Or perhaps there's a good stiff wind blowing against a bank and stirring up the mud or sand. You can be sure to find bass in such areas, looking for an easy meal. If you are fishing in cloudy water, remember that it's a good idea to make your fly, lure, or whatever that bit more visible. Perhaps a fluorescent colour such as neon green or orange would do the trick. Or, try a plug with a really wild action so the bass pick up the vibrations from a good way off.

▼ WATER DISTURBANCE
The vibrations from the plug spread out over many yards and give the bass something to home in on. Still, I should be hiding myself more. Why am I not behind that tree? If a bass is following, it might see me and veer off.

◄ LOOK AFTER YOUR FISH
All members of the bass family are precious, so it makes real sense, when you land one, to keep it in the water ready for a painless release. This beautiful fish was actually taken on a fly, unhooked in the margins, and it's now ready to be slipped back into the main current.

BASS FISHING FROM A BOAT

Being confined to the waterside necessarily cuts down your options, so it won't be long before you want to get out on the water. Once afloat, you can explore all the bass possibilities on the river or lake that you're fishing.

Today's bass fishing boats have aluminium hulls and are fitted with high-powered engines that can really motor you great distances before the bass are fully up and awake.

A top range model will have foot controls so that you can maneuver your boat while your hands remain free for casting and cranking in. Once you get in close, there will be an electric motor just to push you along quietly and smoothly. A graph recorder will be ticking away, scanning the underwater scene and giving you read-outs on any features that you can't see with your Polaroids. You will have a swivel chair that allows you to follow the fish in whatever direction it decides to run. There will probably also be an on-board 'well' or container so you can keep your live bait cool and frisky. And every now and again, your radio will crackle as fellow anglers give you updates on the bass scene around the lake.

One thing is for sure, you'll never, ever tire of fishing for bass. Just when you think you've got the whole thing worked out, there will come a day when you can't do a single thing right, and then you will feel like a real beginner all over again. It's important not to worry, though,

LIVE BAITING

There are times when using some sort of live bait offers the bass angler the best possible chance, especially when you're beginning and fly fishing and spinning can be a little difficult.

1 Live baiting is good when the water is cold and bass are reluctant to expend a lot of energy chasing a lure.

2 Live baiting can also work when the water is very clear. Extreme clarity allows the bass close inspection of a lure, and this often leads to rejection.

3 Minnows, shad, and shiners are excellent bass baits – both alive and dead. They're best in lengths of between 2 and 5 inches. Take great care of your little live fish – keep changing the water around them, and keep them cool. Hook them in the tail. Then watch carefully for a bite. Bass will often take a small fish like this very gently indeed.

4 Crayfish are an excellent bass bait. You'll find them under stones close into the bank. Again, hook them in the tail.

5 Night crawlers are excellent bass baits. You can find them on lawns at night, or dig them up from rich ground. The biggest crawlers are the best. Again, hook them in the tail.

6 Ribbon leeches between 3 and 6 inches in length are also a favoured bass bait. Some tackle dealers sell them. Hook them in the tail again.

7 Grasshoppers and crickets make excellent bass baits. They tend to be thought of as baits par excellence for pan fish, but not always. They are particularly good for smallmouth bass in creeks and streams.

8 Hellgrammites – the larval stage of dobson flies – are tremendous live baits, as are dragonfly nymphs.

9 Frogs and waterdogs are also good but, if you're like me, you just can't bear to use them! As with all live bait, only use them if you think you've got to, and always as gently as you can.

10 Don't forget you'll often need a couple of weights to get the bait down – especially in very hot or very cold weather when the bass are likely to be very close to the bottom.

11 You'll also need a selection of bobbers – what they call floats in Europe. These are both good for registering bites and also invaluable for suspending baits just above the bottom where the bass expect to find them.

⋏ JUNGLE WARFARE

Here I am, up to my thighs in water, searching out every nook and cranny under the branches of a sunken jungle. This is the ideal sort of place for bass to lurk. Plenty of cover, plenty of food – and plenty of opportunity for escape if they make the odd mistake.

when it happens to you, because it's a situation that every angler has to face, not once but hundreds of times in their fishing career. And it's not a complete disaster either. It is simply a lesson telling us that we will never, ever find out everything there is to know about the demanding, yet wonderful, bass – the world's most fascinating fish species.

➤ BASS ON

And the plan worked... for once! A lovely bass came to a very small plug worked just under the surface. There was a boil and a bang, and here I am straining to keep a spirited four-pounder from the tree roots.

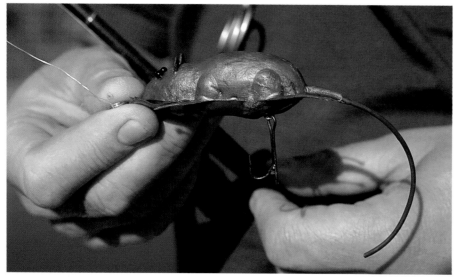

◣ BIG WATER BASS
Bass are often found in very large waters as well as smaller pools and streams. Here, as ever, the whole key is location. Look for bass wherever there are rocks, sunken islands, in-flowing streams – anything that spells food and shelter to this little marauding predator.

◣ GIVE THEM A SURFACE BAIT...
Bass really have an eye to any food source whatsoever, and a floating mouse like this really can cause mayhem if the fish are in the mood. Sometimes, a really calm day is the best. At other times, when there's wind on the water, they'll come up and take a mouse like this with real savagery.

➤ OR TRY A LIZARD.
These slinky little rubber creatures really do look the part in the water. Hook them through the head and feed the body round the shank of the hook so that the point comes out somewhere in the belly or back area. Then cast out, let the little critter sink to the bottom of the pool, and twitch it back. If puffs of silt come up, all the better. It's more than a bass can resist.

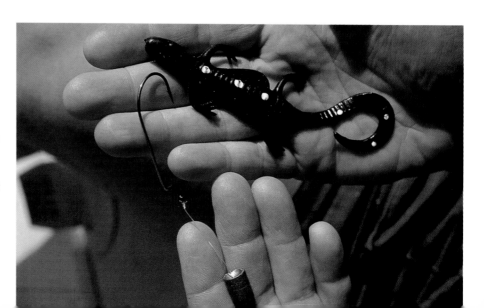

⋏ PINPOINTING THE CAST

Rafa has really sussed out this cast. He's seen the tip of a rock poking through the water surface and he's aiming to cast his rubber jig just over it so that it will sink and can be brought back in the rock's shadow. Extreme accuracy is essential when you're bass fishing.

⋏ FEELING THE JIG DOWN

The cast has been made. Rafa has his fingers on the line, feeling for any tug or interference. If anything seems strange, he'll strike.

⋏ BEGINNING THE RETRIEVE

The jig has hit bottom and Rafa is raising the rod a little bit, feeling for tension in the line. At moments like this a bass can charge in.

THE BASS FISHER'S APPROACH

It's a baking hot day, with a cloudless sky. Fishing for bass is not going to be easy. Rafa has decided that the best way to fish is deep, close to rocks where the bass will be lying, looking for shade and security. Naturally, we're fishing from a boat, as this gives us much better access to all the nooks and crannies that bass love to seek out. There is hardly any wind, so we needn't worry about anchoring up – we're just simply drifting very, very slowly, working huge expanses of water as the morning progresses into afternoon.

Bass fishing is all about searching new areas of water and trying new tricks and dodges to get them to feed. For this reason, the fishing is never dull, but always really sparky and exciting.

⋏ INDUCING A TAKE

Rafa is now lifting the jig through the water, very slowly, erratically, twitching it back trying to make the jig look as alive as possible.

⋏ FINGERS THAT TELL ALL

Those fingers transmit information to Rafa's brain. Any tug, any pull, anything suspicious, he'll know instantly and will strike.

➤ A JOB WELL DONE

This isn't a huge fish, but considering the day – blazingly bright and mill-pond calm– it's a beauty. Some challenge, eh? In the background you can just see the little plastic fish that spelt disaster for our 2 pound black bass.

SEA
FISHING

SEA FISHING

IN AN INTRODUCTION TO FISHING SUCH AS THIS BOOK, I'M AFRAID WE DON'T HAVE THE SPACE TO GO INTO BEACH AND BOAT FISHING IN MINUTE DETAIL. HOWEVER, I WOULD LIKE TO SUGGEST WAYS IN WHICH YOU CAN ADAPT THE SORT OF TACKLE THAT I'VE ALREADY SUGGESTED TO SEA FISHING.

⋏ FRESH FROM THE SURF
A lovely sea bass pictured next to the plug that was its downfall. Bass like this one, around about 5 pounds (2.2kg) in weight, are great opportunistic feeders, combing the shoreline for worms, crabs and any small fish that they can come across. This is why plugs and spinners work so well.

With your ordinary float fishing tackle, carp and pike gear, you can actually have a great deal of fun sea fishing, especially with bass, mullet, flat fish and wrasse. If you find that you enjoy this style of fishing, then you will probably want to take sea fishing a step further and buy all the necessary equipment. You will also find that if you do go out on boats, the skippers will generally look after you, and teach you the rudimentaries of sea fishing very quickly indeed.

Sea sport doesn't come much more exciting than bass fishing. Bass are spread pretty widely around the shores of the Northern Hemisphere, and you can pursue them on most types of beaches, especially in and around harbours, piers and jetties.

Bass come inshore during the spring and early summer, departing for warmer waters in the later autumn. Very occasionally, if the early winter is particularly mild, a few will remain.

SPINNING FOR BASS

Bass are predators, primarily, feeding on any small fish that they can find, and also on marine worms. It makes sense, therefore, to pursue them with either bait or with spinners. We'll look at the bait fishing possibilities on the next page.

Spinning is an active and exciting way of fishing. Choose something silver and about 3, or at the most 4, inches (7–10cm) long.

Travel light and try to cover as much of the shoreline as you can. Don't worry too much about long casting, because you will often find bass feeding amidst the breakers. If the sea is very calm, watch out for bass chasing small fry in the surface regions and aim for these patches of activity. Also, look out for seabirds attacking small fish from the air; you can guarantee that the bass will be there too, attacking from beneath.

⋏ SCANNING THE SURFACE

The sea is a big place and you need one or two pointers if you're going to catch fish such as bass. Perhaps you know where there's an inshore wreck or some rubble left over from a previous building. Perhaps there's a gully, a reef, anything that attracts food and, therefore, bass shoals. Sometimes, you might just see small fish flipping out as they're hunted up to the surface by the fast moving predators.

⋪ A QUICK CAST

If you do see any movement, cast quickly because all fish in the sea tend to feed and move in fast, fluid movements and simply don't hang about. If you delay, you risk missing the shoal. Cast along the beach rather than aimlessly out into the sea... remember that fish are frequently found in the surf itself.

FISHING WITH LIGHT GEAR

Failing that, you can always hunt bass on the bottom with strong carp tackle and a couple of lugworms on, say, a size 2 hook.

Once again, very heavy weights and long casting aren't particularly important, especially if you're out early or late, and the sea is comparatively calm. Again, you will find the bass hunting for food where the waves churn the sand.

In fact, a heavy weight can sometimes be something of a disadvantage, and a light lead does allow those lugworms to drift along with the tide and cover more ground. Of course, you may come across such minor irritations as floating weed and crabs but, believe me, the thrill of a plunging bass on comparatively light gear is certainly one that you will savour.

Like bass, grey mullet come northwards during the warmer months of the year and generally

⋏ UP THE CREEK
Small estuaries and creeks like this frequently attract all manner of fish, especially during the summer. You might find bass, sea trout or the wandering mullet. The incoming tide is often the time to be fishing.

⋎ SAFE IN HARBOUR
Harbours, too, attract a good number of fish – look here for mullet and eels, and for wrasse, bass and sea trout out in the more open water. It's also here that you will meet the skippers willing to take you further out to sea.

⋏ IT'S A BIG WORLD
Here I am fishing amongst the ice flows in western Greenland for halibut. The idea is to lower a huge perk – essentially a metal bar with hooks on – hundreds of feet down towards the bottom where the big fish live.

⋎ BOUNTY OF THE SEA
Although I didn't do too well with my perking (my reel seized up!) these are the sort of fish I was hoping to catch – halibut in the 10 pound (4.5kg) and upwards range. And I mean upwards. There's hardly a limit to the size these fish reach.

arrive around our south coast sometime in May or June, and then spill further north, east and west. In fact, mullet are found in most estuaries and harbours from early summer onwards.

Mullet live and travel in large shoals, often numbering hundreds of fish. They feed on minute organisms in the mud, and you will often see them scraping their lips along the slimy bottom of estuaries. This can mean that bait presentation is a bit of a problem... there simply isn't a hook small enough to take the type of minute foodstuffs that the mullet are foraging for.

Don't despair, however. Mullet quickly become aware of other foodstuffs, especially if they are around human beings for any length of time. This is why harbours can be such excellent places to hunt mullet; the shoals tend to follow the tide and they come in looking for any food scraps that yachtsmen, picnickers and day trippers have left behind.

This is where your float fishing tackle comes in. A 4 or 5 pound (1.8–2.2kg) line, a size 8 hook, with a lump of breadflake on, can prove irresistible in these circumstances.

I remember having great success fishing for mullet in an East Anglian harbour. There was a food canning factory nearby, discarding waste peas and carrots into the water. Guess what bait I used there with great success!?

LUG DELIGHT
A pail full of lugworms dug from the sands at low water. You can buy your lugworm – an ideal bait for flatfish, bass and virtually every sea fish that swims – from a professional digger or, of course, dig your own. But it's hard work... and keep your eye on the tide!

FISHING IN OPEN CREEKS
Mullet out on the open creeks are more difficult, and it often pays to either spin for them with tiny silver spoons, or to use small ragworm on a size 10 hook with a small lead. Once again, try to get to a proven mullet mark as the tide is coming in, and you'll often see the fish working in just 6 or 7 inches (15–17cm) of water. It's exciting stuff indeed. If you find one particular bay that attracts mullet, you can actually put some groundbait in. Place mashed bread in the mud and the mullet will

FISHING FOR MULLET
No fish in the sea is better suited to being fished for by freshwater methods than the mullet. This rig would be at home in the upper reaches of the river, but here in a salty creek, a light float and bread crust work equally well.

find it as soon as there is water cover. Then, simply use bread on the hook with a float as an indicator. Once again, prepare for fireworks.

There's probably no more exciting way of using your freshwater tackle on sea fish than to hunt wrasse amongst the rocks. Wrasse rarely venture far out from rocky outcrops, where they both shelter and feed. These are colourful, hard-fighting fish that will accept lugworm, ragworm, small soft crabs and even take smallish spinners. Fish the bait in mid water, and let it drift around with the swell. Bites are very decisive but put pressure on the wrasse to keep it away from its rocky hideout. Do take care on those rocks; they can be very slippery, especially if they've been covered by the tide and there is a covering of slimy, green weed. It certainly pays to wear a life jacket and fish in couples or threesomes. Some people also tie themselves to the rock as an added precaution. Don't take any risks – not even for a wrasse!

Some of my most enjoyable days have been spent around the coastline. Dawn is my favourite time, when the world is absolutely quiet and an early tide is oozing in through the marshes bringing with it all manner of feeding fish. You leave for home as the first of the holiday-makers are beginning to arrive... knowing that your day is already complete.

THE MARSHES
Marshes can be fascinating places to fish. Obviously, you always stand a chance of mullet, bass, sea trout and eels, but there are some surprises coming the other way. You might find that pike and perch, for example, can live in a saline environment. The answer is to investigate every bit of water that you come across.

◄ MARKS OF THE MULLET
Mullet are very difficult to catch because
they generally feed on minute organisms in
the mud. They capture these by scraping up
the mud with their hard top lips. You'll
often find the marks along soft shorelines
where they've been on the previous tide.
This is a good area to look for them when
the sea comes back in. Try bread, perhaps,
as a starter bait.

SEA CONSIDERATIONS

Fishing the sea calls for all sorts of
extra considerations.

Do take into account what the tide
is doing. It's all too easy to get cut off
on some sandy island by water that's
seeped in behind you. Always keep a
close eye on what the water level is
actually doing. Consult tide tables
and/or the local people before going
out. I've already mentioned that
rocks and cliffs can be particularly
dangerous. This is especially so after
rain, or when the tide has gone out,
leaving rock surfaces slippery. An
incoming tide can also trap you on a
rock ledge unless you have worked
out an escape route. Don't take any
foolish chances.

With the price of lug and
ragworm as it is, it is no surprise
that many people are now digging
for their own bait along sandy beach
areas. However, do check the tides, as
every year diggers are cut off from
safety. Also, make sure that local
regulations allow you to dig in the
area. There are many places where
digging is forbidden. Never dig in
bird sanctuaries or areas of Special
Scientific Interest. It's important
that anglers maintain a good
reputation and good relationships
with local people.

Always wipe down your tackle
with particular care after use in the
sea. The salt can corrode rings, reels
and any other metal parts of
equipment. It's often a good idea to
hose the salt off reels and reel
fittings, for example.

If you've used some spinners in
the sea, then separate them from

◄ BACK-BREAKING WORK
A professional lugworm digger at work. To
fulfil his orders, he's probably going to have to
dig at least a thousand worms during a four or
five hour period. Not much chance to straighten
your back, look around and have a cup of tea.

➤ A VARIED SEASCAPE
This is the sort of view that every sea angler loves to gaze on. The cliffs can offer all manner of fishing close in, whilst the surf-pounded beach can be excellent for bass in the summer and cod in the winter.

your normal freshwater gear. Even if you think you have washed them thoroughly in freshwater upon your return home, there could well still be some traces of salt, and this could corrode your whole collection.

If you are fishing the shore, then you will almost certainly need thigh waders, at least. However, if you can afford them, chestwaders are a much better solution, as they allow you to wade that much further out. With thigh boots, you're always wary of that rogue wave that can splash over the top, soaking you. However, if you do go for chestwaders, always be careful when you are wading. There can be hidden trenches and gullies, so treat every footstep with the utmost caution.

BOAT FISHING

You might very well decide to go out to sea with a skipper in a proper ocean-going boat. It can be great fun… unless you are one of those unfortunate people that suffer from seasickness. My advice is to eat a very careful and modest breakfast. Some people dispute this, but my philosophy is certainly to be better safe than sorry. I always then take a couple of seasickness tablets. Once again, prevention is better than cure… and you can't really cure seasickness anyway – once it strikes, you've had it! Pressure bands that fit on your wrist are said to be effective.

If you are beginning to feel a bit queasy, concentrate on the horizon – a steady focal point helps realign your head and your stomach! And, above all, if you are feeling rough, don't look down. It's also too easy

when you're sorting out a tangle or tying a knot to look at the floor of the boat. If there's anything like a swell, you'll feel ghastly in less than a minute. So take great care when you are doing anything intricate and, if possible, tie hooks well up, even looking towards the sky.

Just because the sea is large, that does not mean there are infinite stocks of fish. In many areas there are very short supplies, so always put back any immature specimens.

⋏ GETTING OUT THERE
It's on boats like these that you'll have to go if you want to hit the offshore wrecks and catch huge numbers of cod, pollock, ling and all the major species that live in deeper water.

Also, exercise some self-control over the mature fish that you catch. For example, if you catch four bass in the morning, how many can you really eat? Take one for the table and return the other three. They're better swimming the sea than deteriorating in a freezer.

MOVING FORWARDS

MOVING FORWARDS

Hopefully, this is a chapter of pure enjoyment, a window on fishing possibilities, designed to inspire you in the future as your angling career develops.

What you've probably already realized is that angling is an extraordinarily broad church, and as a sport it offers hundreds of different opportunities. This, to me, is one of its greatest attractions – there are simply scores and scores of thing to try, limitless skills to learn and a lifetime of experiences to savour. I don't really think there is such a thing as the truly expert angler. True, someone can be very skilled at one particular branch of the sport, but that does not mean to say that he or she will have a clue about something completely different. For example, somebody like Bob Nudd, perhaps the world's top match man,

can land thousands of little fish on a pole during a four hour match, but how would he cope with a 50 pound salmon on a fast-flowing Norwegian river? (Actually, knowing Bob, probably pretty well!)

The one thing that I would advise with absolute sincerity is not to become bogged down in one discipline alone, but to taste as many pleasures as possible. A great many fisher-people become obsessed, most notably, carp anglers. This can mean that all they ever do, year round, decade after decade of their fishing lives, is simply to fish for carp. Now, obviously I love carp too, but to spend the whole of my life fishing for

▲ INDIAN DELIGHT
Can life get better than this... afloat on an Indian river with a knowledgeable guide and the whole day stretching ahead? Mahseer are the target, perhaps the hardest-fighting freshwater fish in the world.

them… never. I've had lots of carp, including some big ones, but while I value my carping memories highly, there are thousands of other moments that I cherish just as much.

Hopefully this book has taught you enough to get going, and pushed you a little along your chosen way. But how far can you really go? Are there any limits to the enjoyment you can get out of this fascinating sport? For example, you might decide to try your hand at match fishing. You'll have to master tackle control, float and ledger tactics alike, learn to use a 10 yard (9m) pole, and even to prepare your own bait. You will find keen competition but great fellowship and a heart-warming

◄ THE MATCH SCENE
It's difficult enough to pit yourself against the fish themselves without worrying about other people. However, match fishing is an important part of the angling scene, especially in Europe.

sharing of knowledge. Join a club at first and enter smaller, closed matches before you think about the bigger, more ruthless opens. Ask for help and advice, and in a friendly club, the chances are that you will receive huge amounts of both. You'll find that your angling career soon hurtles along.

Or, quite differently, you might well decide that salmon fishing is the sport for you. You'll have to cope with 15 or even 16 foot (4.5–4.8m) rods, and master complex sounding casts like the Spey or Half Spey, but you'll find delight in the physical movements themselves. You'll also love the rivers that salmon inhabit – large, clear, pulsating veins of water that crash their way to the sea. And there's something so elemental about salmon themselves, these great silver fish pushing their way from the sea back to their nursery grounds to spawn. If you're going to get started as a salmon angler, try to book as good a beat, at as good a time of the year, as you can afford, and make

⋏ A YARD OF SILVER
Norway – the one time mecca for all salmon fishermen proves that it can still produce the goods. Of course, a lot of our major salmon rivers have experienced problems over the past few years but there's every sign that a general recovery is taking place.

sure that you have a wise and understanding ghillie with you. He will be a man who knows the river intimately, and, if you get on his right side, will probably impart his knowledge with pleasure.

Perhaps you'll want to become a fully-fledged sea angler, spending your leisure time way out from the coast in boats that rock under blue skies. You might fish over wrecks for conger and cod, or you might drift with the tide looking for tope and bass. The sea is a huge place and you'll need sure guidance so, in the early days at least, always try to go out with a skipper who is an expert in his area.

⋖ TROUT AT 10,000 FEET!
This is a photograph of me fishing for trout in Kashmir. The fish, mostly brown trout, were introduced by the British over a century ago, and they've flourished in the cold, clear waters.

149

◄ INDIAN GOLD

This is what mahseer are all about – cunning and with the heart and strength of a bull. This isn't a particularly big fish – they grow to over a hundred pounds (45kg) – but even one like this lets you know you've got a tiger by the tail.

SPECIALIZED FISHING

Many of you will become what are termed Specialist Anglers, people who simply search the world for big fish of every species. This approach frequently demands long hours camped by lakes and rivers, and the fishing can frequently be so slow as to tax anybody's patience. But you will see some stunning fish and enjoy beautiful sunsets and sunrises, with starlit nights between. You will also develop a deep knowledge of the wiles of wise old fish, and you'll soon

▼ STEELHEAD DELIGHT

My old mentor Bob holds up a stunning fresh-run steelhead taken from one of the magnificent rivers in British Columbia.

come to appreciate them and all their secrecy. The specialist world can be a lonely one, but there are groups of like-minded individuals in every part of the country, so it's wise to seek them out and attempt to join.

You might be mesmerized by tying your own flies – many people don't even bother to fish them! You'll delve into the fascinating world of entomology, and you'll collect fur, hair and feather from every imaginable part of creatures from around the globe. This is an engrossing side of the sport, but it pays to begin with the right disciplines, so try to sign up for one of the many night classes that are available round the country.

There are more and more lure fishing nuts around the world today. Perhaps you'll join them and try to catch everything from perch to chub, from bass to sea trout, on surface poppers, mini-lures, rubber lures and lures the world has yet to discover. This fascinating and intricate world is very accessible because it's so new. Everyone is excited, everyone is

swapping knowledge, and I'd advise joining one of the lure societies.

Perhaps you will become a travelling angler. Who could fail to fancy fishing for mahseer in India, taimen in Mongolia, Arctic char in Greenland, or steelhead trout in British Columbia? You'll have huge adventures and meet amazing people in breathtaking countryside.

You'll become an expert at recognizing new birds and butterflies, and identifying the rumble of an elephant or the roar of a panther.

BELUGA!
This is a fabulous beluga sturgeon, caught in the Caspian Sea. And, believe it or not, this was the SMALLEST sturgeon I caught during a week's stay. The average weight was over 200 pounds (90kg) and we actually beached them at over 400 pounds (180kg).

CLEAR STREAM JEWEL
Huge rainbow trout like this one are to be found in the tiny, clear streams of New Zealand. In fact, it is often hard to believe your eyes: how do such big fish exist in such tiny, dancing waters? This fish, typically for New Zealand, was taken on a dry fly.

∧ LOCAL KNOWLEDGE
We can never be the bone fishermen that the locals are. Fidel here knows all about the shallow flat shoreline, the tides, how the fish move and how best to catch them.

∨ AGILITY COUNTS
Amos is also the most agile of fishermen, capable of moving very quickly and quietly through the shallow water in search of the bonefish shoals.

BIG THRILL FISHING
The newly open world of saltwater fly fishing is also beguiling. Imagine the wonder of wading the sun-kissed, crystal clear flats around the Bahaman islands or the Seychelles, fly fishing for bonefish that can pull off a hundred yards of line in that first searing run. Perhaps you'll stalk a permit, one of the great fish of the sea, or strip a lure back for a pike-like barracuda.

The fine bonefish pictured on the right is a prime example of what I've just been talking about. It took Magnus almost four days before he landed this, his first bonefish. But those four days had been brim full of excitement. We'd seen bonefish and tracked them around the coast. We'd seen small sharks come in and harry the shoals. We'd seen barracuda and even, once, a lone passing hermit fish – one of the great treasures of the seas. At night, we'd enjoyed barbecues, watching the stars and moths the size of saucers flying around in the night sky.

And then along came this bonefish, just a yard or so from the shore. Magnus crept toward it on his knees, flicked out a short line, and the fly was engulfed. That bonefish tore more than a hundred yards of line and backing off his reel until the thing literally began to smoke. And then it was landed and it glittered in the sunshine. Those four days of work, watching and learning, were amply rewarded. The pleasure of a challenge satisfactorily completed just could not have been bettered.

≻ BONE ISLAND
Believe it or not, this 8 pound (3.6kg) bonefish took off all the fly line, all the backing and had the angler running through the shallow water after it. It's quite remarkable that fish as small as these can strip reels with such contempt... but they do. If you try to stop them, you do so at your peril.

⋏ TO BOLDLY GO
If you're going to get the very best out of this fishing world of ours, then just occasionally you've got to go for it – even if that means crossing a swaying rope bridge!

⋎ WORLD OF BEAUTY
The dawn mist is just rising off the deserted flood plain, and the river, I know, is full of fish. Another extraordinary experience to pack into my treasure chest of angling memories.

PLANNING AN EXPEDITION
Read everything you can on the place to be visited and, if possible, talk to experts. Consider travelling in a group led by an expert or organized by a specialist company. You'll pay more but your chances of success are much greater.

Don't skimp on clothing or equipment. You don't want to compromise the trip of a lifetime. Take every bit of equipment that you are likely to need, and then some more as well! It's unlikely that there will be tackle shops within a thousand miles of your fishing grounds.

Check all necessary visas and injections. If needed, always take malaria tablets for the prescribed length of time. In warmer climates, and if you are doing a lot of walking, remember to keep well hydrated. Always wear a hat in the Tropics.

Try to learn just a few local phrases such as 'hello', 'thank you', and 'goodbye'. It's a simple matter of common courtesy.

Remember that wild fish are often more easily stressed than those of the park pond. Treat them with every possible measure of respect.

As a leaving gift to your guides, clothing is often more useful than money. Take care leaving medicines unless you make the application and dosage 100 per cent clear.

Remember that to fish magical parts of the globe is a privilege whether you catch or not, so savour every precious moment.

➢ TAIMEN – THE LIONHEART
We couldn't do better than to end on this photograph of the mighty taimen, the lordly, landlocked salmon of central and eastern Asia. Moreover, this magnificent fish is held by two of my greatest Mongolian friends, Gamba and Batsukh, two guys who have looked after me and helped me more than I can say in my journeys over there. Thank you for everything.

GLOSSARY OF KNOTS

I T IS ESSENTIAL FOR EVERY ANGLER TO KNOW HOW TO TIE A SELECTION OF KNOTS. KNOTS ARE USED TO SECURE THE LINE TO THE REEL AND TO JOIN A HOOK OR LURE TO THE LINE. ALTHOUGH THERE ARE THOUSANDS OF DIFFERENT KNOTS, THE BASIC KNOTS ILLUSTRATED BELOW WILL BE SUFFICIENT FOR ANGLING PURPOSES.

HALF BLOOD KNOT

The half blood knot is commonly used for joining hook to line. This type of knot, when tied in nylon line, will not come undone.

▲ STEP 1
Thread the free end of the line through the eye of the hook.

▲ STEP 2
Pass the free end underneath the line and bring it back over the line to form a loop.

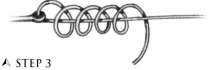

▲ STEP 3
Continue to loop the free end over the line (as step 2) until you have approximately four turns.

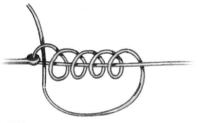

▲ STEP 4
Pass the loose end between the eye of the hook and the first loop.

▲ STEP 5
Pull on the loose end to tighten the knot. Trim off the end.

DOUBLE OVERHAND LOOP

Also known as the surgeon's loop, this knot can be used to create a loop at the end of a fly line, to which a looped leader can be attached.

▲ STEP 1
To begin, double the end of the line back against itself.

▲ STEP 2
Next, tie an overhand knot in the doubled line.

▲ STEP 3
The doubled end should then be tucked through the loop again.

▲ STEP 4
To finish, pull the knot as tight as possible and trim off the end.

BLOOD BIGHT

This knot has similar properties to the double overhand loop. If the end of the knot is not trimmed, several loops can be created to attach, for example, mackerel flies.

▲ STEP 1
Fold the end of the line back against itself (this is known as a bight).

▲ STEP 2
Cross the the doubled end once around the line.

▲ STEP 3
Pass the looped end of the line back through the turn.

▲ STEP 4
Pull the knot tight. Trim off the end of the line to finish.

WATER KNOT

This knot is also known as the surgeon's knot. The water knot is used to join two lines together, for example attaching a lighter hook length to the mainline. The bulk of the knot will stop a sliding bead, and can be useful when ledgering.

⚊ STEP 1

Put the ends of the two lines alongside each other so that they overlap by about 6in (15cm).

⚊ STEP 2

Take hold of the two lines and make a wide loop.

⚊ STEP 3

Pass the ends of the line through the loop four times. Be sure to hold the two lines together.

⚊ STEP 4

Pull the lines tightly so that the loop makes a knot. Trim the two ends.

BLOOD KNOT

The blood knot is also used to join two lines together. As in the water knot, begin by overlapping the ends of the two lines.

⚊ STEP 1

Take one end and twist it four times round the other line. Then pass it between the two lines.

⚊ STEP 2

Repeat with the other free end. Make sure that the first stage does not come undone.

⚊ STEP 3

Wet the knot to lubricate it, then pull it tight. Trim off the two ends.

NEEDLE KNOT

The needle knot shown here can be used to tie solid monofilament to a fly line. More text to be inserted. More text to be inserted.

⚊ STEP 1

Push a needle through the end of the fly line, Heat the needle until the line begins to bend.

⚊ STEP 2

When cool, remove needle. Thread the mono through the fly line and five times around it. Bring the end back and hold it against the line.

⚊ STEP 3

Now take the large loop and bring it several times around the fly line, trapping the mono.

⚊ STEP 4

Pull on alternate ends of the mono to tighten. When the knot is firm, pull the mono tight.

A BRAID LOOP

Although some fly lines are fitted with braided lines for attaching a leader, it is a simple task to form your own from braided mono.

⚊ STEP 1

Push a large-eyed needle into the braid. Thead the braid through the eye.

⚊ STEP 2

Push the needle through the braid until the loose end emerges. A matchstick will keep the loop from closing.

⚊ STEP 3

Adjust the loop until it is the size you require. Cut the loose end until it lies flush, and seal using waterproof super glue.

INDEX

Page references in *italics* indicate illustrations.

A

accessories
    bass fishing 127
    fly fishing 70
angling clubs 21, 22, 149
Arctic char *15*

B

bait 50–51
    deadbait 60, 101, 106–7
    dog biscuits 132
    mullet 141
    plastic 57
    sub-surface 80
bait fishing 40–51
    rivers *86–97*
    stillwaters *76–85*
Baltic pike *60*
barbel *42, 93, 95*
bass *124, 129, 132, 135, 138*
    fishing 124–135
        boat *128*, 132
    largemouth *126*
    live baiting 132
    lures *127*
    sea 138–40
beauty, fish 14–15
behaviour
    anglers 16–17, 144
    flies 118
beluga sturgeon 151
bends 89, 92
binoculars 30
bite 45
    indicators 118
blood bight 156
blood knot 157
boats
    boathouses 79
    fishing 145
    safety 13
bobbers (floats) 43, 45, 46–7, 127, 132
body language 29, 37
bonefish 152, 153

braid loop 157
bread 50, 94, 132
bream *29*, 29, 82–3
bridges 89
brown trout *21, 29, 116, 122*
bubbling 37, 39
buzzers 74–5, 118

C

camouflage 34, *35*
care
    bait 49
    bass 132
    fish 16
    tackle 48, 144–5
carp *22, 29, 32, 37, 38,* 80
casters 50
casting 45, 108–13
casts 65
catfish *49*
char *15*
characteristics, fish 28–9
chestwaders 24, 145
chub *33,* 89, 91, 96
closed seasons 20–21
clothing 24–5
clubs 21, 22, 149
colour
    line 85, 69
    lures 61, 72
    quiver tips 94
comfort 25
cover
    anglers 30
    fish *33,* 78, 89, 101
crease 92
crucian carp *22,* 80
currents 88, 90

D

dams 79
deadbaits 60, 101, 106–7
deep water
    channels 79
    pools 89

double overhand loop 156
drifter float 105
drinks 25
dry flies 66, 73

E

electricity cables 48, 111
equipment
    bait fishing 43
    fly fishing 65
    lure fishing 55
    observation 30–1
expeditions 154
eye protection 111

F

false casting 113
feathering the line 45
feeding terms 37
fish
    care 16
    characteristics 28–9
    feeding terms 37
    holding 23
    seeing 34–5
    signs 38
    see also individual fish names
fishing code 16
flies 65, 73
    choice 116–18
    choosing 69
    storage 70
    tying 74, 151
float rod 43
float tube 127
floatant 65
fly casting 108–13
fly fishing 62–75
    techniques 114–22
    see also flies
fly lines 66, 68–9
footwear 24
forceps 43, 48, 57, 61
free lining 93
fry feeding 37

G

game fishing 16
gear *see* clothing;
    equipment; tackle
glossaries
    bait fishing 45
    bass fishing 127
    fly fishing 66
    knots 156–7
    lure fishing 57
gold heads 74
grayling 15, 70, 88
grey mullet 140–42
groundbait 45, 83

H

half blood knot 156
hiding places, fish 33, 35, 131
hook length 45, 94
hooks 16, 48, 61
    bonnets 61
    flies 69
    removal 16, 97, 103
    storage 48

IJK

induced take 118, 135
inflows 79
islands 33, 79
jigging 57, 59, 105, 128
knots 156–7

L

lakes 76–85
landing net 48
laying-on 81
leader 66, 69
    fly casting 113
ledger weight 45
ledgering 85, 93, 94
licences 21
lie 66
lily pads 32, 79–80

line
    bait fishing 46
    cleaning 113
    floatant 65
    fly fishing 64, 68–9
    lure fishing 57
    rod matching 113
litter 16
lizard lure *134*
location, fish 32–3, 79
lugworms 142, 144
lure fishing 52–61, 151
    techniques 98–107
lures 57, 58–61
    fly fishing 72, 120–21
        bass 127
    plastic 127
    rubber 105, 127

MNO

maggots 50
mahseer 10, 150
mail order 23
marshes 142
match fishing 148–9
mayfly 117
mill pools 88, 90
mouse lure *134*
mullet 140–42
needle knot 157
nymphing 37, 66
nymphs 72, *73*, 118
observation equipment
    30–31

PQ

perch 29, *54, 101, 104, 105*
perking 141
Pheasant Tail 122
pike *21, 29, 37, 56, 60,*
    105, 107
planning 31, 154
plugs 57, 58–9
poaching 17
Polaroid glasses 13, 30,
    111
pole 45
pollution 17
popper 127, 130
power lines 48, 111

pre baiting 45
priest 65, 70
propeller plug *130*
quiver tip 45, 94

R

rafts 91
rainbow trout 29, *68,*
    119, 151
reading the water 38
    rivers 88–9
    stillwaters 82–3
reed beds 78, 79, 80–81
reels
    bait fishing 44, 46
    fly fishing 68
    lure fishing *56*
    storage 48
reservoirs, bait fishing
    76–85
rise 66
rivers 86–97
roach *20, 28–9*
rocks 142
rods
    bait fishing 43–4
    bass fishing 126
    fly fishing 66
    line matching 113
    lure fishing *55*
    storage 48
rubber lures *127*
rudd *28, 28, 34*
rules and regulations 22
run 45

S

safety 13
    fly casting 111
    sea fishing 142, 144
salmon fishing 149
salmon fly 73
sea fishing 136–45, 149
seasickness 145
seasons 20–21, 38
self-defence 35
shoals 28–9, 35
shops 22–3
sight fishing 66
sink and draw method 101

skills 12
smoke screening 37
snap link 57
spawning season 38
spinners 57, 60–61, 139
split shot 45
spoons 57, 60
springs 79
stalking 30, 34
steelhead *68, 150*
stillwaters, bait fishing
    76–85
storage
    flies 70, 75
    lures 61
    tackle 48
streamer fly 73
stress, fish 16
strike 45, 66
    indicators 65, 70
structure 127, 131
sturgeon *151*
surface plug 130
swim 45
swim feeders 42–3, 45,
    48, 84–5
swivel 57

TUV

tackle 12
    bait fishing 42–4, 85, 94
    buying 22–3, 48
    care 48, 144–5
    choosing 46
    fly fishing 64–6
    lure fishing 55
    secondhand 46
    trout fishing 66
taimen 67, *155*
techniques
    fly casting 108–13
    fly fishing 114–22
    lure fishing 98–107
temperature 31
tench *28, 34,* 80–1, *81*
test curve 44
tides 144
tippet 66
touch ledgering 94
trace 57
travel 10–11, 151, 154

trees 89
trolling 57
trotting 45, 92
trout 29, *65, 72*
    brown *21, 116, 122*
    fly fishing 116–23
    rainbow *68, 119, 151*
trout fishing, tackle 66

WXYZ

wading 13, 111
    waders 24, 145
walleye 29
water
    fish signs 38, 82–3,
        88–9
    river conditions 88–90
    safety 13
water knot 157
waterproofs 24
weather, river conditions
    90
weirs 88
wet flies 66, 73, 74
wildlife 11
wind 78, 111
winter
    clothing 24
    fishing 78
    lure fishing 106
wire trace 57
worms 50
wrasse 142
zander 29, 59

ACKNOWLEDGEMENTS

I must first of all thank Mike Taylor, Peter Smith and Mike Smith – at the Red Lion Hotel, The Caer Beris Manor Hotel and Bure Valley Fisheries respectively – for all their help with fishing, filming and photography.

Above all, I would like to thank Johnny Jensen, of Copenhagen, from the bottom of my heart for all his help over the years, both as a travelling companion and as an expert photographer who has lent me his transparencies with unstinting generosity.

I also want to say how much I value the friendship, help and advice given to me by that excellent film cameraman Martin H. Smith. His input to the underwater photography in this book was enormous.

I would also like to thank Steve Gorton for his calm professionalism as photographer on location, and Jo Hemmings, whose powers of motivation and inspiration made this book come together.

Thanks also to Peter and Rafa for all their help in Spain, Batsukh and Gamba for their comradeship in Mongolia, and Pers, Hakan, and all the Danish crew in Scandinavia.

Can I also thank Andy Ashdown for the design of this book, and Carol Selwyn for organising my life and keeping me relatively sane!